RUTH

J. Vernon McGee

THOMAS NELSON PUBLISHERS

Nashville

Published in Nashville, Tennessee, by Thomas Nelson, Inc., and distributed in Canada by Lawson Falle, Ltd., Cambridge, Ontario.

Scripture quotations are from the KING JAMES VERSION of the Bible.

Library of Congress Cataloging-in-Publication Data

McGee, J. Vernon (John Vernon), 1904–1988
   [Thru the Bible with J. Vernon McGee]
   Thru the Bible commentary series / J. Vernon McGee.
     p.   cm.
   Reprint. Originally published: Thru the Bible with J. Vernon McGee. 1975.
   Includes bibliographical references.
   ISBN 0-8407-3261-9
   1. Bible—Commentaries. I. Title.
BS491.2.M37 1991
220.7'7—dc20   90–41340
                                  CIP

Printed in the United States of America
1 2 3 4 5 6 7 — 96 95 94 93 92 91

RUTH

CONTENTS

RUTH

PREFACE

The radio broadcasts of the Thru the Bible Radio five-year program were transcribed, edited, and published first in single-volume paperbacks to accommodate the radio audience.

There has been a minimal amount of further editing for this publication. Therefore, these messages are not the word-for-word recording of the taped messages which went out over the air. The changes were necessary to accommodate a reading audience rather than a listening audience.

These are popular messages, prepared originally for a radio audience. They should not be considered a commentary on the entire Bible in any sense of that term. These messages are devoid of any attempt to present a theological or technical commentary on the Bible. Behind these messages is a great deal of research and study in order to interpret the Bible from a popular rather than from a scholarly (and too-often boring) viewpoint.

We have definitely and deliberately attempted "to put the cookies on the bottom shelf so that the kiddies could get them."

The fact that these messages have been translated into many languages for radio broadcasting and have been received with enthusiasm reveals the need for a simple teaching of the whole Bible for the masses of the world.

I am indebted to many people and to many sources for bringing this volume into existence. I should express my especial thanks to my secretary, Gertrude Cutler, who supervised the editorial work; to Dr. Elliott R. Cole, my associate, who handled all the detailed work with the publishers; and finally, to my wife Ruth for tenaciously encouraging me from the beginning to put my notes and messages into printed form.

Solomon wrote, ". . . of making many books there is no end; and much study is a weariness of the flesh" (Eccl. 12:12). On a sea of books that flood the marketplace, we launch this series of THRU THE BIBLE with the hope that it might draw many to the one Book, *The Bible*.

J. VERNON McGEE

The Book of
RUTH

INTRODUCTION

Ruth is the story of a little foreign girl who came out of paganism
and idolatry in the land of Moab. She came from a people who were in
many senses an outcast people, and she came into a knowledge of the
Lord God of Israel, as Boaz said, "Under whose wings thou art come to
trust" (Ruth 2:12).

Ruth has only four brief chapters, but it is a mighty midget with a
mighty message. In fact, it has several messages. It gives a genealogy
that leads to the Lord Jesus Christ, and it explains His coming from the
line of David. There are commentators who take the position that the
primary purpose of the Book of Ruth is to give the genealogy. While I
agree that this is an important purpose of the book, I do not believe it is
the primary purpose. Keil and Delitzsch make this statement: "The
last words of verse 17, 'he is the father of Jesse, the father of David,'
show the object which the author had in view in writing down these
events, or composing the book itself. This conjecture is raised into a
certainty by the genealogy which follows, and with which the book
closes." The Book of Ruth is very important in connection with the
coming of Jesus Christ into this world. Without this little book, we
could not connect the house of David with the tribe of Judah. It is an
important link in the chain of Scripture that begins with Genesis and
goes right down to that stable in Bethlehem and to the cross, to the

crown, and to the throne of David on which our Lord will someday be seated. This is a very definite reason why Ruth is included in the canon of Scripture.

However, the primary purpose of the Book of Ruth is the presentation of an important phase in the doctrine of redemption. Redemption is possible only through a Kinsman-Redeemer. God could not redeem apart from a Mediator. Since only God could redeem, it was necessary for Him to become that person. Boaz furnishes the only figure for the Kinsman-Redeemer aspect of redemption which is so essential for any proper theory of the Atonement. This little Book of Ruth comes down to our level and tells the commonplace story of a couple who love each other. They were ordinary folk, average folk, and their love story is a mirror in which we can see the divine love of a Savior for you and me. As we proceed into the Book of Ruth, we see this wonderful love story unfold before us.

OUTLINE

Ruth is a very brief book, just four chapters, and there are many ways of dividing it. Some outlines are excellent, but the one we shall follow seems to satisfy the content of the book more than any other. It is the geographical division.

I. In the Land of Moab, Chapter 1

II. In the Fields of Boaz, Chapter 2

III. On the Threshingfloor of Boaz, Chapter 3

IV. In the Heart and Home of Boaz, Chapter 4

CHAPTER 1

Now it came to pass in the days when the judges ruled, that there was a famine in the land. And a certain man of Beth-lehem-judah went to sojourn in the country of Moab, he, and his wife, and his two sons [Ruth 1:1].

This verse that opens the Book of Ruth covers a great deal. In fact, it sounds like modern newspaper reporting. When I was in college I had a job working on a newspaper, the *Memphis Commercial Appeal.* As a cub reporter, I went out with some of the other reporters. Also I got acquainted with the city editor, who was a very nice man, and he attempted to help me all he could. Well, I tried to write up a story of an incident we witnessed one night in Memphis and presented it to the city editor. He read it, just pushed it aside, and said he couldn't use it. Then he told me that there are two things which are always important to get into the first sentence of any article that's newsworthy: the time and the place. In fact, he said, "Get as much in the first sentence as you possibly can." The next time you're reading an important article on the front page of your paper, notice how much information is included in that opening sentence. Sometimes the first sentence is an entire paragraph, and it just about tells the whole story right there. It tells you *what* the incident is, *where* it took place, *when* it took place, and generally *how* it took place.

Now the Holy Spirit of God is a very wonderful reporter. And so in this very first verse He gives the time and the place. The time: "when the judges ruled." Those were dark days. In one sense, they were the darkest days in the history of the nation Israel. You will recall that the Israelites had been in Egyptian captivity, and God had redeemed them by blood and by power, and had brought them through the wilderness. Then He brought them into the Promised Land. And what great promise there was. You would think that this new generation, whose fathers had known the rigors of slavery in Egypt, would serve God in a very wonderful way. But, you know, they didn't.

The Book of Judges tells a sorry and sordid story of a departure from God, of how a people began by serving the living and true God, then turned from Him to idolatry and moral corruption, then how they cried to Him when the enemy oppressed them, and how He raised up judges to deliver them.

I agree with those who are saying right now that America must have revival or she will probably have revolution. Frankly, if you want to see a sweeping revival in this country, don't pray for revival—pray that God will put the church through the fire, and I'll guarantee that will bring revival. It has always brought revival among God's people in the past, and it did in the nation Israel. When they got far from God, judgment came—He sent them into slavery, or an enemy came and defeated them. Then in their suffering they cried out to God. And God was so gracious. He always raised up judges to deliver them.

The Book of Ruth fits into this period of the judges. The incidents that are recorded here take place on this black background of the judges, a time when a man like Samson was a public figure. Today, when scandals have shaken our own country, think of the scandal of a Samson! During the period of compromise, corruption, and confusion, this lovely story takes place. It is light in the midst of darkness. This is the way God writes, is it not? He writes the story of salvation on the black background of sin, and He put this lovely little story on the black background of the time of the judges. This is the picture that we have before us. It is "in the days when the judges ruled."

Not only that, but we're told that the place was Beth-lehem-judah. Now that indeed is very interesting. Beth-lehem-judah has real meaning for a child of God today. And, frankly, Jesus Christ would never have been born in Bethlehem if the incidents recorded in the Book of Ruth hadn't first taken place in Bethlehem. As you sing "O Little Town of Bethlehem," remember that the Christmas story began way back in the incidents which transpired in the little Book of Ruth. These are the incidents that will concern us as we move into this very wonderful portion of Scripture.

The meaning of the name *Beth-lehem-judah* is interesting. Actually, the names in the Bible have a real meaning. *Beth-lehem* means "house of bread," and *Judah* means "praise." That's a wonderful place to live—don't you agree—in the house of bread and praise? The story of Ruth begins and ends there. And that's the place where Jesus was born. Because the names in the Bible, and especially in the Old Testament, have specific meanings, we miss a great deal by not having a translation of the names. I wish we did. At least we have in the notes of certain Bibles an explanation of the meanings of some of the names. It adds a wealth of meaning to the Word of God, as it does in this instance.

"And a certain man of Beth-lehem-judah went to sojourn in the country of Moab, he, and his wife, and his two sons." He lives in the house of bread and praise, but he goes to sojourn in the country of Moab. There's something in the Word of God about Moab that's quite interesting. It's almost humorous. In Psalm 108:9 it says, "Moab is my washpot." Now that's what God says of Moab. You see, these were an outcast people. They had a very sordid and sorry beginning, and Moab just doesn't stand out very well in the Word of God. One way to paraphrase what God says about Moab might be to say, "Moab is my garbage can."

Now will you look at this for just a moment? Here's a family—a certain man, his wife, and his two sons—that goes over to the land of Moab. They leave the house of bread and the house of praise and they go over to eat out of a garbage can. Did you ever hear that story before? I'm sure you immediately will be reminded of the parable that our Lord gave about a prodigal son. He left the father's house in which there was plenty, and he went over to the foreign country, where he longed to fill his stomach with the pods that the swine were eating. I do not think our Lord made up that story. In fact, I do not think He made up parables. I think every parable He gave was a true incident. Probably there were many sons in that day to whom His parable could have applied. And from that day to the present that story has been repeated in literally millions of lives. I talked to a young man here in Southern California not too long ago who had run away from his home in the East. That was his story. He accepted the Lord out here, and we called his father right from my study. How his father rejoiced! That story, my friend, has been lived by many sons.

But here it's the story of a prodigal family. When famine came to the land, they left. They got frightened. Well, their father Abraham got frightened also, and when a famine came to that land during his life-time, he ran off to Egypt. And now here's another famine. This is one of thirteen that are mentioned in the Bible. Every time a famine is mentioned in the Word of God, it's a judgment from God. This is not only the time of the judges with dark days, but these are the darkest of the dark days when this incident took place. They didn't believe God could take care of them in the house of bread and of praise, so they ran off to the land of Moab.

Now I would like for you to get acquainted with this family. It is an interesting family.

> **And the name of the man was Elimelech, and the name of his wife Naomi, and the name of his two sons Mahlon and Chilion, Ephrathites of Beth-lehem-judah. And they came into the country of Moab, and continued there [Ruth 1:2].**

The name of the man is Elimelech. His name means "my God is King" or "the King is my God." Here is a man who has a name that's really meaningful. Just think of the testimony he gave where he worked. When they called him, they didn't say, "Elimelech," in English. They said, "My God is King," or, "God is my King." My, that's a wonderful name to have, isn't it? Why, his very name is a testimony. It's mighty bad, though, to have that name and run off to the land of Moab. He doesn't act as if God is his King.

The name of his wife is Naomi. Now if you were to look up her name in a good Bible dictionary, you'd find that her name means "pleasant." Well, I'd like to give her a really good name. I think her name really was Merry Sunshine. She was a wonderful person. She was the type of individual who always had a very happy outlook upon life. There are many Christians like that today. They always see the bright side. They always register that, and they live above their circumstances instead of being under their circumstances. Some people are always complaining, always finding fault, but not Naomi, not Merry Sunshine.

Elimelech and Naomi have two sons. Their names are Mahlon and Chilion. The name *Mahlon* means "unhealthy," and *Chilion* means "puny." She had two sickly boys. And I imagine Naomi had quite a testimony in Bethlehem because of that. Many people said, "I just don't see how Merry Sunshine can be so radiant and so joyful when she has the burden of those two unhealthy boys." Well, that's her story. And we're told that she and her husband were Ephrathites of Beth-lehem-judah.

"And they came into the country of Moab, and continued there." They not only went to Moab, they made their home there. Now although the prodigal son got into the pigpen, finally he said, "I will arise and go to my father" (Luke 15:18). Sometimes a prodigal stays in the pigpen a long time, and this family, unfortunately, stayed too long. And do you know what always happens to a Christian family—or to an individual who is God's child—which runs off to the far country? They always get a whipping in the far country. You know, that father who received his prodigal son when he came home, could have said to the servant, "Go get me my razor strap. I'm going to whip this boy within an inch of his life. He ran off and spent my money and disgraced my name. I'll teach him." But he didn't do that. He threw his arms around the boy. He told the servant to go kill the fatted calf and to bring the best robe for his son. You see, many Christians today think that God is a very stern, harsh Father and that if you come back to Him, He won't receive you, but He'll punish you. He won't whip you, friend. You'll get your whipping in the far country. That's where the prodigal son got his, and I'll tell you, he got a good one. And this family here is going to be taken to the woodshed. They're going to get a whipping in the far country.

But they are, I think, a fine family. "My God is King" is the father, the head of the family. And there's Merry Sunshine, the wife and mother, and then there are the two sickly boys, Mahlon and Chilion. They go to the land of Moab—they go to eat out of the garbage can and they continue living there.

Notice what happens.

And Elimelech Naomi's husband died; and she was left, and her two sons [Ruth 1:3].

I told you they were going to have trouble in the far country, and they did. It always happens. John says, "There is a sin unto death" (1 John 5:16). I do not know what the sin unto death is for you. For Ananias and Sapphira it was a lie to the Holy Spirit. I don't think that's a sin unto death today. If it were, we'd be very busy conducting funerals in the church. But I don't think it's the same for every Christian. When you get away from God, that's when trouble comes.

Now the husband died. Notice what happened after he died.

> **And they took them wives of the women of Moab; the name of the one was Orpah, and the name of the other Ruth: and they dwelled there about ten years [Ruth 1:4].**

Now the very minute they did that they broke the Mosaic Law. You see, having gotten out of fellowship with God and going to the far country, the next step is always in apostasy; it's to continue on in sin, and even to multiply it. And that's what they did. They broke the Mosaic Law and took wives of the women of Moab.

Orpah means "deer" or "fawn." It means she was the athletic type. And you wonder why an athletic type of girl married one of these sickly boys. But she did. After meeting Orpah, we come to the one we're really interested in: Ruth. And I could give you about ten different meanings for the name *Ruth*. It means "beauty"; it means "personality." And she had this characteristic—she was beautiful but she was not dumb. She is a remarkable person, and I hope that you're going to fall in love with her because she happens to be one of the ancestors of Jesus Christ. In other words, in His humanity, He had the blood of Ruth flowing through His veins. We're going to get acquainted with her. She married Mahlon in the land of Moab. There is a word I'd like to use to describe her, but Hollywood and the high-pressure publicity of our day have spoiled it. It would be *glamour*. Certainly, in the best sense of the word, that would apply to Ruth. And why she ever married this sickly boy is difficult to understand at first, but I think we will understand it later on.

Now this prodigal family is in the far country. Trouble has already come to them, and more trouble is going to come to this mother and wife. She has lost her husband, and her two sons have married women of Moab.

> **And Mahlon and Chilion died also both of them; and the woman was left of her two sons and her husband [Ruth 1:5].**

Now I was expecting that, by the way. I didn't think that they'd make it through another hard winter, and they didn't. And these two boys, Unhealthy and Puny, died. Now she has lost her entire family, and all she has left are two little daughters-in-law, foreign girls. That's all she has. I tell you, trouble did come. And the prodigal family, like the prodigal son, got their whipping in the far country.

Then she arose with her daughters-in-law, that she might return from the country of Moab: for she had heard in the country of Moab how that the LORD had visited his people in giving them bread [Ruth 1:6].

The famine was over back in the Promised Land, and there was bread again in Bethlehem, the house of bread and praise. And so now she wants to return home. It's interesting. The prodigal family and the prodigal son will long for the father's house. And if they don't long for the father's house, they just don't happen to be the children of the father. The prodigal son will never be happy in the pigpen. He just wasn't made for a pigpen. He hasn't the nature of a pig. He has the nature of the father, and he will eventually say, "I will arise and go to my father." Now the pigs love pigpens. There is a story that Peter gives to us in 2 Peter 2:22, which I call the parable of the prodigal pig. ". . . The sow that was washed [has returned] to her wallowing in the mire." You see, one of the little pigs got all cleaned up and told the prodigal son, "You seem to be sold on going home, and I want to go with you." And so the pig went home with the prodigal son, but he didn't like it up there—clean sheets on the bed and a clean tablecloth—ugh! He told the prodigal son, "Why don't we put the food in the trough and all of us jump in and have a big time? And why do we have to have clean sheets? I like mud better." And finally the little pig said he'd arise and go to his father. And you know where his old man was—down there in the pigpen. And the prodigal pig went back to the pigpen; he always will. And the prodigal son will always go home, friends. You can depend on that. But today it's confusing. On the freeways of life there are prodigal sons going to pigpens and prodigal pigs going up to the father's house, and they ought not to be. Sometimes they get into the church, and they start causing trouble. Like a pig when he gets into the father's house, he starts causing trouble in the church. He's a troublemaker, but eventually he'll end up back in the pigpen. You just have to wait, you see.

So eventually this family must go home. Finally Naomi says she's going back to Beth-lehem-judah.

> **Wherefore she went forth out of the place where she was, and her two daughters-in-law with her; and they went on the way to return unto the land of Judah [Ruth 1:7].**

Now Naomi is going to talk to her daughters-in-law just like a Dutch uncle. She's going to tell them what the situation is going to be when they get to Bethlehem. You see, the Moabites and the Israelites just didn't have anything to do with each other. Israelites had no dealings with the Moabites, just like later on they didn't have any dealings with the Samaritans. Now here Naomi tells them that because they're Moabites, it's going to cost them something to go up with her to Bethlehem. They'd never be able to marry again, and these were young women. It would mean perpetual widowhood and poverty for them because she had lost all of her property.

> **And Naomi said unto her two daughters-in-law, Go, return each to her mother's house: the LORD deal kindly with you, as ye have dealt with the dead, and with me [Ruth 1:8].**

Now she had a wonderful word for them. They'd been good daughters-in-law. And you know, it's difficult for a mother to feel that any girl is worthy of her son. But here's one who could say of these foreign girls that they had made good wives. But she encourages them to return and go back to their own mothers and not to go up with her because of what it would cost them. And she says,

> The LORD grant you that ye may find rest, each of you in
> the house of her husband. Then she kissed them; and
> they lifted up their voice, and wept [Ruth 1:9].

This is truly a womanly scene. Naomi tells them that if they stay in the land of Moab, they can remarry among their own people; but if they go up with her, they wouldn't have a chance. Here are these three women standing in the crossroads in the land of Moab. When I visited the land of Moab, I thought of these three women. Around any bend of the road there in that wild country, on those roads that twist and turn, you might be able to see these three, Ruth and Naomi and Orpah. There they stand, and they're weeping. They have their handkerchiefs out, and I call this the meeting of the handkerchief brigade. They're all weeping.

> And they said unto her, Surely we will return with thee
> unto thy people [Ruth 1:10].

Now their first decision was, "We'll go with you."

> And Naomi said, Turn again, my daughters: why will
> ye go with me? are there yet any more sons in my womb,
> that they may be your husbands? [Ruth 1:11].

You see, the Mosaic Law said that when a man died, the nearest of kin was to marry his wife, and if there were a brother he was the one to marry her. This was a very strange law indeed, and we'll see it later on here in the Book of Ruth because this is the story of the kinsman-redeemer. So here Naomi just talks turkey to them. She tells them how it is. "If you go with me, you can never get married. My people couldn't identify themselves with you. It'd be too costly. You'll really be outcasts because we don't have any dealings with the Moabites."

Turn again, my daughters, go your way; for I am too old to have an husband. If I should say, I have hope, if I should have an husband also to night, and should also bear sons [Ruth 1:12].

And so Naomi urged them to stay in their own land. She made it very plain. She said, "Even if I had more sons, which I never will, but if I did, would you wait for them to grow up? Why, you'd be robbing the cradle. You wouldn't want to do that."

Would ye tarry for them till they were grown? would ye stay for them from having husbands? nay, my daughters; for it grieveth me much for your sakes that the hand of the LORD is gone out against me [Ruth 1:13].

You see, God had judged Naomi's family, and she told them they'd have to bear that. She didn't want them to go with her for that reason.
   Now here we go again.

Any they lifted up their voice, and wept again: and Orpah kissed her mother-in-law; but Ruth clave unto her [Ruth 1:14].

Now we come to the parting of the ways. As I said, you might come around the curve in any road in Moab and see these three women. And had you and I gone by, my friend, in that day and seen these three women in eastern garb weeping there, we would have thought that nothing of importance was taking place. But, my friend, I'll tell you

how important it is: the decision made there will determine whether
Jesus Christ will be born in Bethlehem or not. And if the right decision
is not made there, you might as well send word to the wise men not to
come, because He won't be born there. It may not look important to us,
but a tremendous decision was made there. We find that Orpah kissed
Naomi, but Ruth clung to her. Orpah turned back, and that's exactly
what Naomi said for her to do.

> **And she said, Behold, thy sister-in-law is gone back
> unto her people, and unto her gods: return thou after thy
> sister-in-law [Ruth 1:15].**

Orpah made the decision to go back. Her decision for God had not
been real, you see. She goes back to idolatry. And when she goes back,
she walks off the pages of Scripture into silence and into oblivion. We
never hear of her again. But Ruth made a decision for God, and when
she made this decision, it was for time and eternity. And you'll find
her mentioned in the very first chapter of the New Testament. She's in
the genealogy that led to Christ. Naomi wants to test her to see if she's
genuine or not. She told her to go back to her gods, to go back with her
sister-in-law.

> **And Ruth said, Entreat me not to leave thee, or to return
> from following after thee: for whither thou goest, I will
> go; and where thou lodgest, I will lodge: thy people
> shall be my people, and thy God my God [Ruth 1:16].**

She made an important decision there. It's a sevenfold decision, and
it's a decision for God. And this is what I believe is genuine repentance, friend. This is the kind of repentance that means something.
That's exactly what the New Testament says. Second Corinthians 7:10
says, "For godly sorrow worketh repentance to salvation not to be re-

pented of: but the sorrow of the world worketh death." Ruth made this decision. She continues,

> **Where thou diest, will I die, and there will I be buried: the LORD do so to me, and more also, if ought but death part thee and me [Ruth 1:17].**

Now that's Ruth's sevenfold decision, and it's a real decision for God. I want you to notice this because this is very important in this day when believers make a great deal of their dedication to God, and they promise God a great deal, but they don't carry through with it. I believe God holds us to it. What we need today are folk who make *real* decisions for God. The decision of Ruth was that kind of decision.

First of all, Ruth said, "Whither thou goest, I will go." In other words, she's saying to Naomi, "I made a decision to go with you, and I'm going with you. I'm not using this as a passport just to get into Palestine." And the second phase of her decision is, "And where thou lodgest, I will lodge." In other words, she would not only go with Naomi, but she'd also identify herself with her. "I accept your poverty." She bears the same name now, as she had married Merry Sunshine's son, and she will stick right with Naomi. Her third statement, "Thy people shall be my people—I'm forsaking my people, idolators, and I'm identifying myself with God's people." And, friend, you can't make a decision for God unless you identify yourself with God's people. It'd just be impossible to do otherwise, you see. And Ruth knew that. She said, "You say I'll be an outcast. All right, I'll be an outcast, but thy people will be my people." And then the fourth, "Thy God my God." Now I can explain why this girl Ruth decided to marry that unhealthy boy that moved into the neighborhood who'd come from the house of bread and praise over in the Promised Land. The reason, I think, is evident. For the first time she heard of the living and true God. She met a family that knew the living and true God, and she

married into that family because she had come to know the living and
the true God. "Thy God will be my God." What a decision she had
made! And not only that but, "Where thou diest, will I die." That is
more meaningful to Ruth than it would be for you and me today. What
she's saying is this, "The hope of Israel is my hope." You see, the Isra-
elite believed that someday he would be raised from the dead to live in
that land. That was the hope of Abraham. He never believed that he
was going to heaven. He believed he would be raised from the dead
right down here, and that's the reason he bought the cave of Machpe-
lah and buried Sarah there, and he himself was buried there. Isaac had
that same hope, and even old Jacob, who died down in the land of
Egypt, said he wanted to be buried back up there where his fathers
were buried. This was because they had a hope of the resurrection of
the dead. They were seeking "a city . . . whose builder and maker is
God" (Heb. 11:10), which will be a reality on this earth someday.
That's the Old Testament hope. When the Lord Jesus said to His disci-
ples in the Upper Room in John 14:2, ". . . I go to prepare a place for
you" *away* from this earth, that was brand new, you see. God's promise
to Abraham was to give him an eternal home on this earth. And Ruth
said not only that where Naomi died she would die, but also, "And
there will I be buried." You see, her hope is in that land—just as the
hope of Abraham, Isaac, and Jacob had been. She had now the Old
Testament hope. Then the seventh part of her decision is this: ". . . The
LORD do so to me, and more also, if ought but death part thee and me."
What a decision she'd made! She said, "I didn't make this for just a
day or for an hour. I made this decision for time and for eternity."

What we see in Ruth is genuine and real repentance. We hear a
great deal today about repentance, and the average notion is that repentance means shedding a few tears. You will recall that 2 Corinthians
7:10 says, "For godly sorrow worketh repentance to salvation." Note
that repentance is not salvation; it *leads* to salvation. ". . . But the sorrow of the world worketh death." What is the sorrow of the world?
Well, it's to shed tears. The worldling can shed tears. Now look yonder

at the crossroads again with these three women there. Orpah shed just as many tears as Ruth did. Her handkerchief was just as damp as Ruth's was. What's the difference between these two women? The difference is quite obvious. Orpah shed a great many tears, but hers were not tears of real repentance. What is real repentance? The Greek word used in 2 Corinthians 7:10 is *metanoia*. It means "to change your mind." It means to be going in one direction, then to change your mind, turn around, and go in the other direction. A lot of people come to a place where they're under conviction, and they intend to change— or at least they say they do—and they shed a few tears, but they keep right on going the same way. And that's exactly what Orpah did. She shed the tears right along with Ruth, but she didn't turn around and go to Bethlehem and make a stand for God. No, she went back to idolatry. And a lot of folk are like that today—they just shed tears. Tears are not repentance, friend, although they may be a by-product of repentance.

My dad used to tell about a steamboat which plied on the Mississippi River years ago when he was a boy. He said it had a little, bitty boiler and a great big whistle. When this boat was moving upstream and blew its whistle, it would start drifting downstream, because it didn't have enough steam to do both. There are a lot of folk like that today. They have a great big whistle and a little, bitty boiler. They have never come to a saving knowledge of Christ. Oh, they'll shed a lot of tears over their sins—they blow their whistle—and they're very emotional. They love to give testimonies full of emotion, but their lives don't measure up. I know several men who can make people weep when they get up and give their testimonies. They have tears in their voices, but I wouldn't trust those men at all. I don't think they're bornagain men at all, just emotional. They are like Orpah.

During my ministry I have learned to put less confidence in tears than I formerly did. I found out that these sob-sisters today can shed tears, but they don't really make a decision. Sometimes a person can be dry-eyed and make a decision for Christ, and it's genuine and real.

Years ago when I was a pastor in Pasadena, two couples came forward on Easter Sunday morning. One couple blubbered all over the place. They cried and wept so that we couldn't make any sense out of what they were saying. But they made a big impression on the officers who thought this couple was really genuinely saved. They were not. I pulled them out of two cults, and the pastor who followed me told me he did the same thing. The other couple was dry-eyed. Because they didn't shed a tear, one of the elders called me aside and asked, "Do you think they're converted?" Well, that's been at least twenty-five years ago, and every now and then I see that couple, and they're still standing for the Lord. Let me just ask you a personal question: Did you really make a decision for Christ, or did you just shed a few tears? Tears themselves are meaningless, and the sorrow of this world worketh death, friend, and that kind of repentance is no good. But repentance that is genuine is not to be repented of. It will lead to salvation, and you'll be genuinely converted—as was Ruth.

Ruth makes a real decision for God. She says, "I accept the poverty. I accept being an outcast. I also accept the fact that I will remain a widow the rest of my life." She was willing to accept all of that in order to take a stand for God. She makes her decision to go back to Bethlehem with Naomi.

Now Merry Sunshine knew Ruth—

When she saw that she was stedfastly minded to go with her, then she left speaking unto her [Ruth 1:18].

She knew that when this girl made a decision, it was a real decision, it would stick; so she didn't need to say anything else to Ruth.

And so we follow them.

So they two went until they came to Beth-lehem. And it came to pass, when they were come to Beth-lehem, that

all the city was moved about them, and they said, Is this Naomi? [Ruth 1:19].

Now they have returned. The prodigal family is coming home, but it's not a family now. Actually, it's just this widow Merry Sunshine, who doesn't look like Merry Sunshine, and a little foreign girl by the name of Ruth. And the people of the city ask, "Is this Naomi? Is this Merry Sunshine?"

And she said unto them, Call me not Naomi, call me Mara: for the Almighty hath dealt very bitterly with me.

I went out full, and the LORD hath brought me home again empty [Ruth 1:20–21a].

Now I do not know too much about mathematics, but I do know this: it's a long way between being full and being empty. Having zero and having everything is just about as far apart as you can put figures—or put anything. On one hand, empty; on the other hand, full. She went out full; she comes back empty. Friend, may I say this, if you're a child of God, you have been blessed with all spiritual blessings in the heavenlies, and you have everything in Christ. When you go out from His presence and lose your fellowship, you're going to find out something. You're going to find out that you get your whipping in the far country and you're going to come home empty, and I mean *empty*. But, thank God, when you come home that way, just like the prodigal son did, you'll find the Father waiting to receive you with outstretched arms. He'll bless you in a way that He's never blessed you before. He'll be very good to you. That's the thing that happened to the prodigal son. A robe was given to him, a fatted calf was killed for a banquet—all of this for the boy who returned home.

Now Naomi had told her friends to call her Mara, Gloomy Gus. She says,

> **Why then call ye me Naomi, seeing the LORD hath testi-
> fied against me, and the Almighty hath afflicted me?
> [Ruth 1:21b].**

You'd think maybe they would change her name to Gloomy Gus, but they didn't. And the Spirit of God leaves it that way also. "So *Naomi* [not *Mara*] returned." The Spirit of God says that she's going to be Merry Sunshine again.

> **So Naomi returned, and Ruth the Moabitess, her
> daughter-in-law, with her, which returned out of the
> country of Moab: and they came to Beth-lehem in the
> beginning of barley harvest [Ruth 1:22].**

This is a good time to arrive in Bethlehem. We have left the land of Moab, and in the next chapter we'll be going into the fields of Boaz near Bethlehem.

CHAPTER 2

And Naomi had a kinsman of her husband's, a mighty man of wealth, of the family of Elimelech; and his name was Boaz [Ruth 2:1].

Here we have Boaz introduced to us, and he is actually the hero of our story. He will be the one who will set before us the type of the kinsman-redeemer—but that's a little later. Notice that immediately he's identified as a kinsman of her husband. That is important to note. "And Naomi had a kinsman." I can't pass that by without saying that Boaz is a picture and a type of the Lord Jesus Christ. And it can be said of you and of me that we have a Kinsman also, one who was made like we are, yet sinless—"holy, harmless, undefiled, separate from sinners" (Heb 7:26). He is the one who is able to save us to the uttermost. The name *Boaz*, by the way, means "strength." He was a mighty man of wealth. And I'm told that you can also translate it "a mighty man of war." And it could be said "mighty man of Law" also. All three were true of Boaz. He's a mighty man of war; he's a mighty man of wealth; and he is a mighty man of the Law. He is the one we're introduced to now. He was of the family of Elimelech.

And Ruth the Moabitess said unto Naomi, Let me now go to the field, and glean ears of corn after him in whose sight I shall find grace. And she said unto her, Go my daughter [Ruth 2:2].

We find here one of three very strange laws; that is, they are strange to us because we haven't anything in our legal system today that corresponds to them. To glean grain or other produce was part of the Mosaic system. This was God's way of taking care of the poor, and Ruth and Naomi are very poor. The very fact that Ruth says she wants to go and glean is indicative of their poverty.

Now we want to look at this strange law. It is stated in several places. For instance, we have it in Leviticus 19:9–10: "And when ye reap the harvest of your land, thou shalt not wholly reap the corners of thy field, neither shalt thou gather the gleanings of thy harvest. And thou shalt not glean thy vineyard, neither shalt thou gather every grape of thy vineyard; thou shalt leave them for the poor and stranger: I am the LORD your God." You see, God told His people that they had to take care of the poor, and do it in this very unusual way. God didn't put them on relief. He didn't have an anti-poverty program that just gave them money. God did it, I think, in a very sensible way. They had to go and glean. The law is directed, you see, to the landowner. It is stated again in Leviticus 23:22: "And when ye reap the harvest of your land, thou shalt not make clean riddance of the corners of thy field when thou reapest, neither shalt thou gather any gleaning of thy harvest: thou shalt leave them unto the poor, and to the stranger: I am the LORD your God." And then the final reference is in Deuteronomy 24:19: "When thou cuttest down thine harvest in thy field, and hast forgot a sheaf in the field, thou shalt not go again to fetch it: it shall be for the stranger, for the fatherless, and for the widow. . . ." It was God's way of taking care of the poor people of that day. He didn't put them on relief; He didn't get them in a bread line; He didn't make them recipients of charity. He gave them something to do. They had to work for what they got. They could go into the fields and glean, and they would have to do it by hand. It's not like it is today in our country. Doing it by hand is not very efficient. The harvesters leave a great deal of the grain in the field, up to thirty percent. Once they'd gone through the field God wouldn't let them go back over it the second time. He said, "After you've gone over it the first time, then the poor can come in and glean." I think God's method is a good one. Of course, it's not up-to-date to fit into our modern, political economy, but God's method certainly worked in Ruth's day when thirty percent of the grain was left in the field. They tell me that there is a McCormick reaper now out in Kansas that cuts the grain and at the same time threshes it and sacks it up. If it drops just one little grain of oats or wheat, there's an arm that reaches down, picks it up and puts it in the sack. They don't miss a thing today! This was God's marvelous provision for the poor in a day when the poor were not even considered at all. And, friends, God is concerned for the poor. The Word of God has been the only thing that has given the poor man a chance. You go throughout the world and check that out for yourself. A great many of us today in this country are enjoying the benefits of those in the past who have labored, and we have entered into their labors. We are greatly blessed as a people. But many of you can remember when we were poor. I was a very poor boy myself, and you may have that background also. We owe a great deal to the Word of God, because it is only the Word of God that has ever given the poor man a square deal. The politicians won't, I can assure you of that. They are only after votes; they're not after the poor man's welfare. But God is, and this was God's marvelous arrangement.

And so Ruth acts upon this law which seems so strange to us today. She came under both categories, the stranger and the poor. She asked Naomi to let her go and glean, and Naomi told her to go.

And she went, and came, and gleaned in the field after the reapers: and her hap was to light on a part of the field belonging unto Boaz, who was of the kindred of Elimelech [Ruth 2:3].

And if you'd seen Ruth going out that day down the road from Bethlehem, you would have seen a girl who had no idea into which field she should go. How is she going to find her way into the field of Boaz? It's going to be very important that she get in that field. If she doesn't, then you can tell the wise men that there's no use coming to Bethlehem. Jesus won't be born there. And you can tell the shepherds to stay with their flocks on the hillside because He won't be born in Bethlehem. You see, it's important that she go into the right field. How is she going to find the right field?

When I was in Bethlehem, I took a walk myself. I may not have walked down the exact road that Ruth did, but it couldn't have been very far from it. And I thought of her as I walked. I think we've located the fields of Boaz. They're right down at the foot of the hill from Bethlehem. Bethlehem was a typical city in Palestine of that day. All of them were built upon a hill, and this little town of Bethlehem was no exception. Evidently down at the foot of the hill in a very fertile valley were the fields of Boaz. When Ruth went out of Bethlehem that day, she had no notion where to go. Now Scripture says, "Her *hap* was to light on a part of the field belonging unto Boaz. . . ." Well, the word *hap* is an old Anglo-Saxon word, coming from the same stem as *perhaps* or *happens*. Her "hap" was just a happenstance, as we call it today. From her viewpoint, it was just by chance. Actually, it was just that. Now this brings us again to the question: How did she find her way into the field of Boaz when it was so very important that she go into the right field? Did God put up a stop and go sign, a red and green light, or point an arrow into the right field? He did not. Well then, did a voice speak out of heaven? No, no voice spoke out of heaven. Well, she must have had a vision, someone thinks. But she didn't have a vision. Well, how in the world is this girl going to get into the right field? Let's ask Ruth. I would say to her, "Ruth, I'm sure that you had some pretty definite leading about the field of Boaz." And she'd say, "No, I didn't. You'd better go back and read the Book of Ruth again. It says that my *hap* was to light on his field. I just happened to go in there." May I say to you, from the human viewpoint, it was just happenstance. From God's viewpoint, it's something else. He's going to lead her into the right field. But He's not going to lead her in the way a lot of people talk about it today.

Some folks talk about God's will as if they'd just had a Western Union telegram from Him or a Special Delivery air mail letter from heaven. My friend, God doesn't lead that way today, and I don't think He has ever led very many that way. Back in the Old Testament He led some in a very direct manner, but Ruth was not one of them. It seems to me that Ruth's decision was more important than some other decisions that were made. God said to Jonah, "Arise, go to Nineveh" (Jonah 1:2). And He told Jeremiah and Ezekiel to speak out. But I want to say this to you: what He told these men to do is not nearly as important as Ruth's getting into the right field, because Jesus' birth in Bethlehem is dependent upon her going into the right field. Now God is going to overrule in all of this, and God is going to guide in the background. That's the wonderful thing about the Lord's will. I'm not sure that it's necessary for God to give you and me a road map. Sometimes I wish He would. And I hear some people talk today as if they *have* a road map. They say, "The Lord's will was for me to do this, and I knew this was the Lord's will." I wish I could be that clear, that sure.

Years ago, when I was a pastor in Cleburne, Texas, I received two calls from other churches, one to the east of Texas and the other to the west in California. And I didn't know which to take. I'm being honest with you. I actually got down on the floor and cried out to God to show me which call to accept. He didn't. I had no vision. But then I heard Dr. Harry Ironside make the statement that of the decisions he had to make in his life, eighty percent (I think this is the figure he gave) were made without knowing at the time they were God's will. He did not know until sometime later on. After hearing that, I went back home and told my wife that the atmosphere had all cleared, that I felt we were to go to California. I wasn't sure, but I felt that was the way I was to move.

As far as God's will for your life is concerned, if you think that He's

going to put up a green light for you at every corner or an arrow pointing or a voice out of heaven, you're just wrong. He doesn't do it that
way. And when I hear people say that, I just know there's something
radically wrong with them, or they're trying to kid somebody. But wait
just a minute—Dr. Ironside said that afterward he knew whether it had
been God's will or not. And I think that sometimes God does let us go
down the wrong road. "But," somebody is going to say, "you could
make a pretty bad decision." You sure can. But the interesting thing is
that if you have two ways before you and you take the wrong way,
there's nothing in the world that'll keep you from coming back and
starting over again. And you can be sure of one thing: If you had two
ways to choose from and chose the wrong way first, then you *know*
which is the right way. It's amazing today how many people interpret
God's will as being the easy way. Well, it's not always the easy way. It
certainly wasn't for Ruth.

If you'd asked Ruth if she knew she was going into the right field,
she would have said, "I don't know what you're talking about." And
had you asked her why she chose the field she did, I think she would
have said to you, "I prayed about it. Before I left home this morning, I
asked God to lead me. I really didn't know which road to take, but I got
down here and looked into one field with nice grain but there weren't
many poor people gleaning in it, so I was pretty sure that whoever
owned that was a skinflint. But over on the other side of the road, my,
there were a lot of poor people gleaning. And I knew that man must be
a generous man, and I needed to find that kind of field because I'm a
Moabitess, a foreigner, an outcast, and I didn't want to be put out; so
that's why I chose this one." And I suppose that when she'd gone a
distance down the road, and probably hesitated a minute, that the
angels on the battlement of heaven looked over and held their breath.
They said, "My, I hope she goes into the right field." She went into the
right field. And I think that all heaven heaved a sigh of relief when
they saw her going into the fields of Boaz. God is overruling. For Ruth

there was the element of uncertainty, but on the other side there was the providential dealing of Almighty God.

One of the glorious things, as we go through this world today, is to know that our times are in His hands; to know that He is ordering the events of this universe; and to know that God has said that nothing can come to a child of His without His permission. You must remember that there was a hedge around Job, and even Satan couldn't touch him until God gave permission. God will not give permission unless it serves some lofty and worthy purpose. It did serve a lofty and worthy purpose in the life of Job. And I'm sure that Ruth did not realize the significance of the decision she was making. She just went in, and I think she prayed and had a reasonable basis for it. For the child of God today who is frustrated because he's looking for some sign, some experience, some light, some voice, some vision, some dream, he must realize that God is not speaking to us in that way today. God today is speaking to us through His Word. And the child of God who walks in fellowship with God, with no unconfessed sin in his life, and has not grieved the Holy Spirit, can commit his life to God. And when he gets to a place where he isn't clear just what God's will is for him, he can make a decision and move into the situation. Now maybe he makes a wrong decision, but God has permitted it for a purpose. As I look back on my life, there is one instance where I expected God to open up a door for me, and He didn't open up that door. In fact He slammed the door, as it were, in my face, and I felt very bad about it. But I thank God that He did it, because now I can look back and see that it was best. It's like what Joseph said to his brethren when they came to him after the death of old Jacob, their father. He said in Genesis 50:20, "But as for you, ye thought evil against me; but God meant it unto good." How wonderful that is, and may it be an encouragement to you today. Perhaps you are actually biting your fingernails and are wondering why you don't get clear leading. You know Christians who act like they have a hotline to heaven. Now it's wonderful that all of us have access to God, but I'm not sure that He always talks right back to us. So let's be very careful today about the way we banter about the statement, "I know this is the Lord's will." We just can't always be sure. But we can commit our way to Him, have no unconfessed sin in our lives, not grieve the Holy Spirit, and be in the center of the Lord's will as best we know. Yes, my friend, you can commit yourself to Him in a wonderful way. And even if you got into the same predicament that Joseph did, or even that Job did, say with him, "Though he slay me, yet will I trust in him" (Job 13:15). My friend, that's the glorious truth that brings a joy and an expectancy to life. The providence of God makes every day a thrill for the child of God. I'm glad that He didn't give me a blueprint because, frankly, I like to take a trip over a new road, going into an area I've never been before. I did that one autumn when we were in the Ozarks. My, how that road twisted and turned. And every twist and turn was a thrill—the autumn leaves were a riot of color. Nature seemed lavish, covering every hillside with polychrome pictures. And I'm so glad that God didn't send me pictures of it all ahead of time. What a thrill life can become for us!

> **And, behold, Boaz came from Beth-lehem, and said unto the reapers, The LORD be with you. And they answered him, The LORD bless thee [Ruth 2:4].**

Now for some unexplained reason, Boaz was detained from getting to his fields early in the morning. He was a prosperous man, and maybe he didn't have to be there early. But I judge by the character of the man that he was on top of every situation, and he probably had business that morning in Bethlehem. Perhaps he had to wait until the First National Bank of Bethlehem opened so he could get the payroll for his workers. But whatever the reason may have been, he didn't get out into his field until a little later.

Notice what he did when he got out there. He said to the reapers,

"The Lord be with you." That's capital speaking. And they responded, "The Lord bless thee," and that's labor answering. Say, that doesn't sound like some of the labor leaders and capitalists of our day, does it? It doesn't sound like the steel workers or the steel owners either. Unfortunately, capital and labor both are very far from God today. Now, frankly, I am a poor preacher, and I'm not a capitalist. My dad was a working man. I remember him in overalls most of the time because he was a hard worker. I just can't sanction godless capitalism today. From listening to them, I get the impression that most of the labor leaders are very godless. I don't take sides today. I just wish that we could get something of real Christianity, the real born-again type, into this area. It would certainly help the relationship. You'd hear language like this: Capital: "The Lord be with you." And then labor answering: "The Lord bless thee." My, what a marvelous capital/labor relationship existed there in the fields of Boaz!

> **Then said Boaz unto his servant that was set over the reapers, Whose damsel is this? [Ruth 2:5].**

Now we have really come to the part of our story that is exciting. This little foreign girl by the name of Ruth, willing to accept poverty and ostracism and perpetual widowhood, is out in the field gleaning. By chance, she has gone into the fields of Boaz, the most acceptable bachelor in Bethlehem. I suppose that the mothers of marriageable daughters in Bethlehem had given many a tea or invited him over for a meal. They say the way to a man's heart is through his stomach, and I imagine many had tried that route. But somehow or other he hadn't been interested in the local girls. But then one day he goes into his fields and he sees for the first time this little widow from Moab. And I tell you, he falls for her! Now our King James translation here is rather stilted. Don't misunderstand me—I still feel that the King James translation is our best for public use. Although the American Standard Version of 1901 is probably more accurate, it's very hard to improve on this King James. But there are places where I think we can bring it up to date, and this is such a place. What Boaz said here is not quite, "Whose damsel is this?" May I just give you several very free translations? He says, "Well, where in the world has she been that I haven't met her before?" That's very free, as you can see. Or let me give it another way. Perhaps as accurate Hebrew as you can possibly get, could not be translated, but would sound like a Hebrew wolf whistle. He fell for this girl. This is love at first sight.

And maybe you're wondering if I believe in love at first sight. May I say to you, I believe in it very strongly. I proposed to my wife on the second date we had. The reason I didn't propose to her on the first date was because I didn't want her to think I was in any hurry. Now don't get any ideas if you're a young person. It was a year before we got married. We wanted to make sure. Yes, I believe in love at first sight, but I think love ought to be tested by quite a bit of time before marriage takes place.

Boaz had a case of love at first sight. This man really fell for Ruth, and this is romance in the fields of Boaz, if you please.

> **And the servant that was set over the reapers answered and said, It is the Moabitish damsel that came back with Naomi out of the country of Moab [Ruth 2:6].**

His foreman tells Boaz who she is and implies, "Why, you certainly wouldn't want to know her. She just came in the fields here." And I think he's halfway apologizing and assuring Boaz that he had nothing to do with her coming into the field. He explains:

> **And she said, I pray you, let me glean and gather after the reapers among the sheaves: so she came, and hath continued even from the morning until now, that she tarried a little in the house [Ruth 2:7].**

Although it's very clear to us that Boaz has fallen for this little foreign girl, his superintendent didn't see that at first, and he seems quite apologetic. "This Moabitish woman came out here and asked to glean, and I couldn't turn her down. After all, the Mosaic system permits her to come in here and glean since she's poor and a stranger." But he didn't need to be apologetic, because Boaz has fallen in love with this girl. And this reveals a great deal about Ruth, of course. It reveals that she certainly lived up to her name. As you'll remember, we did not attempt to translate Ruth into any English word because I do not think there is any one word that will quite describe her. *Ruth* means "beauty, personality," and we suggested the word *glamour*, but that word has been absolutely ruined by Hollywood and by cheap literature today so that I just don't know what word to use. But this scene reveals something of the attractiveness of this woman. What all the other girls and beauties of Bethlehem had not been able to accomplish, this girl did— and she didn't even try at all. She had already taken her position as an outcast, and she did not expect any attention at all. You'll notice her surprise when she finds out that she has attracted the attention of this man.

Now after his superintendent has apologetically given him the information he wanted, notice the reaction of Boaz. He turns and addresses Ruth.

> **Then said Boaz unto Ruth, Hearest thou not, my daughter? Go not to glean in another field, neither go from hence, but abide here fast by my maidens [Ruth 2:8].**

Now let me pause and say that this is strange language. Here is a man that honestly would not want the poor in his fields. The Mosaic Law said he had to permit it. And I think Boaz was generous, but he just didn't put up a sign and say to the poor, "Come in and glean." And he didn't invite them in. But here is an occasion when he goes out of his way to urge Ruth not to go into any other field to glean. "I want you to glean in my field." Well now, is he interested or *is* he interested? Also, he adds,

> **Let thine eyes be on the field that they do reap, and go thou after them: have I not charged the young men that they shall not touch thee? and when thou art athirst, go unto the vessels, and drink of that which the young men have drawn [Ruth 2:9].**

There are two things here that are very important. He not only invites her to stay in the field, but he also puts around her his cloak of protection. He says, "I have now given orders that you can come into this field, and that you will not be hurt or harmed in any way." Frankly, in that day it was very dangerous for a woman in Ruth's position—a widow, a woman from Moab. She was likely to have insult upon insult heaped upon her. And not only that but she would not be safe. And Boaz, recognizing that, immediately puts his cloak of protection around her.

It was almost as unsafe on the roads of Bethlehem in that day as it would be today on the streets of our modern cities. One of my missionary friends from Africa put it like this, "It is safer on the jungle trail in Africa, where I minister, than it is on the streets of Los Angeles." Now that's what civilization has risen to, and especially this new civilization with its liberal approach to crime. It's the cry-baby type that says that the poor criminal is to be brought back into society and is to be reclaimed. May I say to you, the whole point (and we need to get back to it) is to punish the criminal. That was the purpose of putting one into prison. It wasn't intended to do anything else but to punish him. And how much reclaiming are they doing today? May I say to you, that type of thinking is almost a farce today. God knows this because He knows the human family, and He knows you and me. He knows that you and I today have an old nature, and until you and I come to Jesus Christ, we can't be reclaimed, my friend.

Now will you notice Ruth's reaction to this very noble and generous gesture on the part of Boaz.

Then she fell on her face, and bowed herself to the ground, and said unto him, Why have I found grace in thine eyes, that thou shouldest take knowledge of me, seeing I am a stranger? [Ruth 2:10].

When I first wrote my book *Ruth, the Romance of Redemption*, I assumed and took the position that here Ruth was actually being either naive or a coquette, that she was playing it rather cleverly by asking, "Why have I found grace in thine eyes, that thou shouldest take knowledge of me, seeing I am a stranger?" Now, frankly, I can't hold that position any longer. She is not being that at all. You see, she had been properly warned and made aware of her situation if she returned to Bethlehem with Naomi. And that's the reason the other woman of Moab, Orpah, didn't come. Orpah just wouldn't make the sacrifice. She was not willing to be a perpetual widow and be poverty-stricken the rest of her life and be ostracized besides. Therefore, she remained in the land of Moab. But Ruth came, realizing all of that. When she went out into the fields of Boaz, she never dreamed that anyone would ever take any notice of her. In fact, she expected that they would all turn their backs upon her, because the Jews at this time didn't have dealings with the Moabites. As we'll see later on, even the Mosaic Law shut a Moabite out from the congregation of the Lord. The Moabites had a very bad beginning that's not very pretty to recount. And for that reason they are given this very low position. But this little Book of Ruth reveals something that is quite interesting: racial barriers *were* broken down, and God is concerned and loves even those who have upon them a stigma and a judgment.

Such is the picture of you and me today. ". . . While we were yet sinners, Christ died for us" (Rom. 5:8). And Paul says you just don't find love like that in this world today. Only God has a real concern for

people. You just don't find love anywhere else like the love God shows
for sinners. But here is an exhibition of it, and that's the reason Ruth
says, "Why have I found grace in thine eyes?" She's absolutely star-
tled. She's a stranger, an outcast. And I think it's an honest, sincere
question she's raising. She can't understand this breaking over of a
racial barrier. Here is an interest that she did not expect.

Now I can answer Ruth's question very easily. If she would just go
home and look in a mirror, she'd see the reason. She's beautiful. She's
lovely. She's attractive. She has everything that is desirable in a woman
and a wife, and for that reason this man has fallen in love with her. I
can answer her question.

But there is a question I cannot answer: Why have I found grace in
the eyes of God? Now don't tell me to go home and look in the mirror,
because I've done that. Frankly, friend, the image is something that's
not quite attractive. I don't see the answer in the mirror. But God has
extended grace toward us. And there are those who consider the theme
of the Book of Ruth to be just that. The grace of God is exhibited here in
the grace that was manifested to this woman. And I must concur to the
extent that this is certainly a marvelous example of grace. You and I
both can ask Ruth's question as we come to God: Why have I found
grace in Thine eyes? We cannot find the answer within ourselves;
we're not lovely; we're not beautiful to Him; we are not attractive; we
do not have those qualities that God adores and that He rewards and
respects. We're sinners, and we're in rebellion against God. And yet,
in spite of all that, God loves us! That is one of the great truths of the
Word of God. He *demonstrated* that love, because "while we were yet
sinners, Christ died for us." He extended His grace to us. And, friend,
that's the basis upon which He saves us today. He hasn't any other
reason for saving us.

**And Boaz answered and said unto her, It hath fully been
shewed me, all that thou hast done unto thy mother-in-
law since the death of thine husband: and how thou hast**

left thy father and thy mother, and the land of thy nativity, and art come unto a people which thou knewest not heretofore [Ruth 2:11].

Probably the reason Boaz had not met Ruth when she accompanied Naomi back to the land was that he was away on one of those innumerable campaigns that were carried on during the times of the judges. You'll recall that Boaz could be described not only as a mighty man of wealth but also as a mighty man of the Law and a mighty man of war. Undoubtedly he was a soldier. So he evidently was out of town and, when he returned, he heard this buzzing about a widow who had come back with Naomi.

The things they were saying about her were quite good. Now Bethlehem was evidently given over to gossip, as most places are, and they were gossiping about this foreign girl, but what they were saying was good, which was unusual. They were amazed at her. They said, "Imagine! This little foreign girl has come back, and she's true to her mother-in-law. She didn't desert her when she got here. She doesn't chase around after the men, and she is a wonderful person." Boaz just couldn't believe that in addition to all he had heard about her character she was as attractive as she was. But now when he sees her and finds out that all of these qualities are wrapped up in one person, I'll tell you, that's the reason that he has fallen for her. Just listen to him as he realizes that tremendous sacrifice she has made.

The LORD recompense thy work, and a full reward be given thee of the LORD God of Israel, under whose wings thou art come to trust [Ruth 2:12].

She had come to trust the Lord God. This is the reason she had left the land of Moab and made that radical decision. She had said that the God of Naomi would be her God. She had turned from idolatry to the living and true God. This woman has come to trust God; she was one of His children. Therefore this is the wonderful testimony that she had there in the land of Israel. And Boaz says, "May a full reward be given to you. May you be recompensed for this decision." And if Boaz has anything to do with it, he's going to see that she gets a full reward, and he begins immediately to work toward that end. He's in love with her, friend, and he is going to redeem her. She needs to be redeemed.

> **Then she said, Let me find favour in thy sight, my lord; for that thou hast comforted me, and for that thou hast spoken friendly unto thine handmaid, though I be not like unto one of thine handmaidens [Ruth 2:13].**

Ruth's reaction here is interesting. She hadn't expected any comfort. She hadn't expected to be spoken to in a friendly manner. And the reason she didn't expect any of this was that she was not like one of his handmaidens. And that was probably the reason he *did* notice her—she wasn't like the other girls. You know, today we're living in a society that talks a great deal about being an individual and having your own thoughts. Some time ago I had a bull session with a group of college students. They wanted to have it, and I met with them. That's the age when tremendous things are taking place in their own hearts. They are in rebellion because they're pulling loose from old ties. God made us that way purposely, by the way, but we won't go into that. These young people were talking about being individuals, making their own decisions, and being different. And do you know what? Every one of them looked alike. They wore their hair alike, they wore the same type of clothing, and they expressed themselves in the same way. I couldn't help but just sit there and laugh. They wondered why I was enjoying it so. It's interesting to hear people talk about how they want to be different, and yet they want to be exactly like the crowd. But, you see, Ruth was different. And that's the reason Boaz had fallen in love with her. Some of us should want to be a little different—not necessarily in dress—but we need to be different in other ways. If you're a child of God you *are* different. Talk about doing your own thinking—it's the child of God who thinks differently from the crowd. He has to. Christians are a minority group.

But now let's look in on Boaz and Ruth again. My, he has invited her to lunch! Can you imagine that? We think of those days as being more or less uncivilized. They were not in the jet set back in that day. But he meets her about ten o'clock in the morning, invites her to lunch, and she has lunch with him the same day. My friend, you can't improve on that, can you, even in our day?

> **And Boaz said unto her, At mealtime come thou hither, and eat of the bread, and dip thy morsel in the vinegar. And she sat beside the reapers: and he reached her parched corn, and she did eat, and was sufficed, and left [Ruth 2:14].**

I want to ask again: Is Boaz interested in her? My, I'll tell you, he has fallen in love with this girl, and he'll make every effort now to make her his wife. We'll find that there was a big hurdle in the way.

> **And when she was risen up to glean, Boaz commanded his young men, saying, Let her glean even among the sheaves, and reproach her not:**

> **And let fall also some of the handfuls of purpose for her, and leave them, that she may glean them, and rebuke her not [Ruth 2:15–16].**

He even says to his workmen, "I want you to show her every courtesy and consideration. Now you let her glean even among the sheaves." You know, the poor would be very apt to try to get up to where the grain was good, and you can well understand that the owner of the field would have to keep them behind his reapers. But Boaz said, "You let her come up and glean right where you're reaping." And Boaz was a man of the Law. Because he knew what it said, he instructed his men not to go back and pick up a sheaf if they happened to drop one. Now he's even going one step further. He says, "When you see that Ruth is gleaning immediately behind you, when nobody is looking, you just drop a sheaf back there and go on. When she gets up to it, she'll call, 'Yoo-hoo, you dropped a sheaf.' You just tell her you're sorry but you can't go back and get it, and for her to keep it."

> **So she gleaned in the field until even, and beat out that she had gleaned: and it was about an ephah of barley [Ruth 2:17].**

An ephah was a bushel. The value of it would be a pretty good day's wage, especially for this little widow.

> **And she took it up, and went into the city: and her mother-in-law saw what she had gleaned: and she brought forth, and gave to her that she had reserved after she was sufficed.**
>
> **And her mother-in-law said unto her, Where hast thou gleaned today? and where wroughtest thou? blessed be he that did take knowledge of thee. And she shewed her mother-in-law with whom she had wrought, and said, The man's name with whom I wrought today is Boaz [Ruth 2:18–19].**

When Ruth brought in this tremendous amount of grain, Naomi said, "My, I've never seen anything quite like this! Where have you been today? Somebody has shown undue consideration for you." And so Ruth just tells the whole story to Naomi. And up to this point, actually, Ruth still doesn't know exactly who Boaz is, but Naomi does.

And Naomi said unto her daughter-in-law, Blessed be he of the LORD, who hath not left off his kindness to the living and to the dead. And Naomi said unto her, The man is near of kin unto us, one of our next kinsmen [Ruth 2:20].

The Hebrew *goel*, or "kinsman-redeemer," is the second law that is so strange to us because we do not have anything that corresponds to it. But it was God's provision for taking care of His people. You see, God gave the Law for a land and for a people. The Mosaic system was a marvelous system for that day and for that land.

Ruth certainly went into the right field, for this man was a near kinsman. And here in the Book of Ruth we see the law of the kinsman-redeemer in operation. Now you do not always see the Mosaic system in operation in Israel, but this little book highlights for us the law of the kinsman-redeemer, as well as the other two laws which we've mentioned that are very strange to us. One of them is the basis on which God took care of the poor. It was an unusual way. God would permit them to go into the fields and the vineyards and glean after the owner had sent his reapers and gatherers through one time. It was a marvelous way because a great deal was left. I had the privilege several years ago of holding meetings up in Turlock, California, right after the grape gathering had taken place. The owner of a very large vineyard found out that I liked grapes, and he told me just to go out into his vineyard and help myself; so the pastor and I went out there. He told us they had already gathered the grapes, and that we were welcome to whatever was left. Friends, if I'd had a ten-ton truck, I'm sure I could have filled it up with the grapes that were left there! We would look up under the vine and, my, some of the biggest, finest-looking, luscious bunches could be found. I told the pastor, "You and I are gleaning, and I think we fulfill our rightful place because we're poor preachers, and we're exercising that which is part of the Mosaic system." God's way of taking care of the poor preserved their dignity by giving them an opportunity to work for what they received.

Now here in our story of Ruth we encounter the law of the kinsman-redeemer. It is stated for us in Leviticus 25, and it actually operates in three different areas. It operates in relation to the land and in relation to individuals and in relation to widows.

Now Boaz was related to Naomi's husband, this man whose name was Elimelech (which means, "My God is King"). I take it that Elimelech's and Boaz's fathers were brothers, which made them cousins, and therefore we could also say that Boaz was cousin to Ruth's first husband. So Naomi tells Ruth that Boaz is one of their next kinsmen.

Now there's an emphasis upon this Hebrew *goel*. What does that mean? Well, let's look at this law in relationship to the land. "The land shall not be sold for ever: for the land is mine; for ye are strangers and sojourners with me. And in all the land of your possession ye shall grant a redemption for the land" (Lev. 25:23–24). Now how would God do this? "If thy brother be waxen poor, and hath sold away some of his possession, and if any of his kin come to redeem it, then shall he redeem that which his brother sold" (Lev. 25:25). This is the law of the kinsman-redeemer in relationship to land. Now let's see that in operation. When these people came into the land, God gave them the Promised Land; it was theirs. But they occupied it only as they were faithful to God. When they were unfaithful, God put them out of the land. He said, "The land is Mine, but I give it to you as a pemanent, perpetual possession." He gave them title to it, and they still have title to it, by the way. God put them in the land according to tribes. A certain tribe had a certain section of the land. You may have maps in the back of your Bible which show the division of the land among the tribes of Israel. And each family within each tribe had a particular plot of land. He could never leave it. But suppose he becomes poor. Perhaps he's had two or three years of crop failure. (Famine did come because of their unfaithfulness to God.) And a man has to get rid of his land. Now he has a rich neighbor who sees the opportunity to take a mortgage. Well,

all he can take is up to a fifty-year mortgage, because in the Year of
Jubilee every mortgage is cancelled, and the land returns to its original
owner. This law kept the land in a family. But it's a long way between
jubilees. A man may be middle-aged at one jubilee, and in another
fifty years he'll be gone. So if he had sold his property he would not
get it back in his lifetime, but his son would get it. Now suppose he
has a rich relative, a cousin for example, and that rich cousin is moved
toward him and wants to help him. Well, that rich cousin can come
right in and pay the mortgage off, and restore it to the owner even before the Year of Jubilee. And I assume that in the Year of Jubilee whoever did the redeeming was also remunerated for whatever he'd put
into the land. That was God's method. It would be wonderful to have a
rich uncle, wouldn't it? It'd be wonderful to have that kind of a redeemer.

Now this applied not only to property but also to persons. "And if a
sojourner or stranger wax rich by thee, and thy brother that dwelleth
by him wax poor, and sell himself unto the stranger or sojourner by
thee, or to the stock of the stranger's family: After that he is sold he
may be redeemed again; one of this brethren may redeem him" (Lev.
25:47–48). Now a man may have been in very unfortunate circumstances. He not only lost his property, but perhaps due to drought and
famine in the land, his children are hungry and he sells himself into
slavery in order to feed his family. This poor fellow will be in slavery
until the Year of Jubilee. If that year is forty-nine years away, that's
going to be a long time to be in slavery. He may live and die in slavery.
But suppose again that he has a rich relative, and one day he sees that
rich uncle coming down the road, taking his checkbook out of his
pocket. He says, "Look, I don't want my nephew to be in slavery," and
he pays off the price of this man's slavery. He has redeemed him, you
see, and the man can go free.

The kinsman-redeemer is a picture of the Lord Jesus Christ. He is
our Kinsman-Redeemer. And that's the reason the word *redemption* is
used in the New Testament rather than *atonement*. Atonement covered

up sins, that's all. But redemption, friend, means to pay a price so that the one who is redeemed may go scot-free. Now Christ not only died to redeem our persons, He died also to redeem this earth. You and I live on an earth that someday is going to be delivered from the bondage of corruption, and there'll be a new heaven and a new earth. That is part of His redemption.

The only biblical example of a kinsman-redeemer is that of Boaz, which is the reason I wrote on the Book of Ruth. It reveals the love side of redemption. Here is a man who is a kinsman-redeemer, but he doesn't have to act in that capacity. We'll find out there's another kinsman who was actually a nearer relative than Boaz, and he had the opportunity to take action, but he turned it down. He doesn't care for Ruth but, you see, Boaz loved her. That makes the difference. Now God didn't have to redeem us. We were lost sinners. If He did not redeem us, He could still be a just and holy God. But He loved us. You see, salvation by redemption is a love story. And now we have it told here in simple language illustrated by this little foreign girl from Moab and Boaz in the land of Israel.

> **And Ruth the Moabitess said, He said unto me also, Thou shalt keep fast by my young men, until they have ended all my harvest.**
>
> **And Naomi said unto Ruth her daughter-in-law, It is good, my daughter, that thou go out with his maidens, that they meet thee not in any other field.**
>
> **So she kept fast by the maidens of Boaz to glean unto the end of barley harvest and of wheat harvest; and dwelt with her mother-in-law [Ruth 2:21–23].**

That took about six weeks. For six weeks, every afternoon, you'd see coming into Bethlehem—not wise men, not yet; not shepherds, not yet; not Joseph and Mary yet—Boaz and Ruth. Boaz is in love with

Ruth. I think he looked like a dying calf in a thunderstorm. And the little town of Bethlehem is gossiping, good gossip, "Our most eligible bachelor has fallen." And I'm sure that Naomi with whom Ruth lived could look out the window and see them coming in every afternoon. She knows something needs to be done about this, because actually Ruth is in a most unique position. Boaz is in love with her, and he wants to redeem her.

It's wonderful to have a Savior who loved us, who came to this earth 1900 years ago in order that He might redeem us.

CHAPTER 3

THEME: On the threshing floor of Boaz

In this chapter we're on the threshing floor of Boaz. It's obvious that Ruth was not claiming what she had a right to, and so Naomi takes over. As we shall see, she is a regular matchmaker. Ruth stands in a most unusual position. And to understand what is taking place in this chapter, it's necessary, I think, to understand the third of the Mosaic laws that we encounter here—which is so strange to us. We have seen two of them already, and now we're introduced to the third. Also we must understand the threshing floor of that day and the significance of it. To understand that is essential.

Now if you think the laws we've looked at so far were unusual, you just look at this one: "If brethren dwell together, and one of them die, and have no child, the wife of the dead shall not marry without unto a stranger: her husband's brother shall go in unto her, and take her to him to wife, and perform the duty of an husband's brother unto her. And it shall be, that the firstborn which she beareth shall succeed in the name of his brother which is dead, that his name be not put out of Israel. And if the man like not to take his brother's wife, then let his brother's wife go up to the gate unto the elders, and say, My husband's brother refuseth to raise up unto his brother a name in Israel, he will not perform the duty of my husband's brother. Then the elders of his city shall call him, and speak unto him: and if he stand to it, and say, I like not to take her; Then shall his brother's wife come unto him in the presence of the elders, and loose his shoe from off his foot, and spit in his face, and shall answer and say, So shall it be done unto that man that will not build up his brother's house" (Deut. 25:5–9). Now I think you'll agree, friend, that this is an unusual law! As far as I know, the little Book of Ruth gives the only illustration of it in Scripture, but it must have been enforced many times because it was put in force when a man died childless.

Now here's the situation. Suppose there is a man living in the hill country of Ephraim, known today as Samaria. Suppose he has several sons. One evening one of the boys gets down the lantern, polishes it up, trims the wick, and that night when it gets dark he lights the lantern, and he starts down the road whistling. One of the brothers says to the others, "I wonder where in the world he's going." The others say they don't know. So late that night they hear him coming down the road whistling again. He comes in, and he doesn't say anything. They don't ask anything, but they're wondering. The second night he does the same thing and, believe me, they're curious by now. So they make a few inquiries the next day. The third night when the boy takes off and then returns, his brothers are waiting for him. They say to him, "Where have you been?" "Oh," he says, "I've been down the road." And they say, "We understand that there's a new neighbor moved in down there." He says, "Yes, there is." And one of the brothers says to him, "We understand that they have a daughter." And he says, "Yes." They ask, "Is it true that you've been down there to see her?" And he says, "Well, I've been trying to put the good neighbor policy into practice so I've been down there visiting with them, yes." Well, they say, "We'd like to ask specifically, have you been to see the girl?" So he says, "Well, to answer specifically, I have." Then they say, "We want to be personal. Are you interested?" And he says, "Yes, I am, to be very honest." And they say, "Well, we've taken a good look at the girl, and we don't like her. We feel like we ought to have a family huddle because if anything happens to you, it means that one of us will have to marry the girl." According to the Mosaic Law she could claim one of them, you see, if she'd had no children. That was the provision. And the boy says, "Well, I'm going to marry her because I asked her tonight to marry me and she has agreed to it." "Well," they say, "we feel like you ought to go through the clinic. We hope you're healthy, because we're just not going to marry her. We're not interested in her." Now suppose this boy goes ahead and marries the girl, then he takes sick and dies, or he's gored by a boar, or a tree falls on him, or he drowns in the Jordan River, or he's killed in battle. What about that? Well, she is a widow now, and she can go immediately and claim one of these brothers. And, believe me, he's going to have difficulty turning her down. Now suppose he just stands to it and says, "I warned my brother. I told him not to marry this girl, and I just don't want to marry her." Then she can bring him into court. If he refuses to take her to wife even in court, she can step up to him, take off his shoe, and spit in his face! Friends, that meant he was disgraced, and a man is not apt to go that far.

So you can see, here is an unusual law which puts a childless widow in a most unique position. It changes her position altogether. She now can claim one of the brothers. In fact, that's her duty to her dead husband. Well, frankly, I can well understand that this is something that tied the families together in that day. It made every member of the family interested in who brother Isaac was going out to see since the other brothers were always involved in a situation like that.

This law was God's provision. And there were two objectives He had in mind that are obvious here, and there may be others. The first is that He wanted to protect womanhood. You can understand that if her husband died and left her with a farm and a vineyard and a flock of sheep, she would have difficulty. So she could claim immediately a brother or the nearest kinsman, and he'd have to make this decision. The Law was to protect womanhood. Now I've heard the criticism made that the Bible is a man's book. Well, my friend, when anybody makes that statement, it is evident he hasn't read the Book very carefully. Sometimes you wonder if the man has a chance—he doesn't have a chance here, that's for sure.

Now the second reason for this law is that God wanted to protect land rights. God not only gave to the nation Israel the land of Palestine, He not only gave to each tribe a particular section of that land, but He also gave to each individual family a particular parcel of land. Each family had their own land. As we have seen, a family could lose their land. But in the Year of Jubilee it would automatically return to the original owner. However, a widow might go out and marry some stranger who would gain ownership to the property. And so, you see, God protected that property. The nearest of kin had to be the one to marry her in order to make it possible to retain the title of the property in the nation and in the tribe and in the family. Now it seems to us like a very strange law, but apparently it was one that worked in the land of Israel.

In the case of Ruth, she's a widow without any children, and the property which belonged to her husband has been lost because she and Naomi are poverty-stricken. She has a perfect right to claim Boaz since he is a near kinsman. And as Naomi has already indicated, he is a kinsman-redeemer. The fact of the matter is, this man Boaz is sweating it out. His hands are tied. He cannot claim her for his wife. It's Ruth's move. She has to claim him as her husband. A little later on we'll find out that there happens to be another kinsman who is actually nearer than Boaz, and Ruth could claim him if she wanted to. Boaz doesn't know which one she'll claim. Therefore, Boaz must wait until Ruth makes the move. Because Ruth is not making the move, Naomi takes charge and tells Ruth, "You've got to let this man know that you want him as a kinsman-redeemer."

Now we're going to see a very strange procedure. In order to understand it, it is necessary to understand the threshing floor of that day. You see, God made a wonderful provision for these people. Since they were an agricultural people, a great many of the laws pertain to agriculture. The Mosaic system was not only for the people of Israel, but also it was for that land. It was adapted in a very particular and peculiar way to the land which we know as Palestine. Therefore, we find here a law that relates to the threshing floor and the practices of the day. Customarily a threshing floor was located on top of a hill to catch any wind that was blowing in order to blow away the chaff. It was in the opposite position from a winepress which was located at the bottom of a hill, because it was easier to carry the grapes downhill than to lug them uphill. The winepress, you'll remember, was the place where Gideon was, as he was threshing grain. The reason he was down there threshing was because he was hiding it from the Midianites who had impoverished Israel. The angel of the Lord appeared to him—don't tell me God doesn't have a sense of humor—and addressed him, "Thou mighty man of valour" (Jud. 6:12). And there's Gideon down at the winepress, scared to death, when he should be up on top of the hill. You can imagine his frustration as he pitches that grain up into the air, and with no wind blowing down there at the bottom of the hill, the chaff and grain come back down around his neck. I think he was very discouraged. Then when the angel of the Lord appeared to him and said, "Thou mighty man of valour," I think Gideon looked around to see to whom He was talking. When he didn't see anybody else he turned to the angel of the Lord and said, "Who? Me? You don't mean to tell me that you think that I'm a mighty man of valour. I'm one of the biggest cowards you've ever seen." Friend, that's what he was. But thank God, God can use a coward who is dedicated to Him. And when this man was dedicated to the Lord, he could overcome the Midianites with only three hundred men. What an encouragement that ought to be to many of us today. Although the story of Ruth also takes place during the era of the judges, apparently it was at a time when Israel had returned to the Lord. Remember that while Naomi was still in Moab, she had heard that the famine (which was God's judgment) was over. Israel had probably returned to an era of tranquility, and the threshing floor was in its proper place at the top of a hill.

But now let's look at the threshing floor. The clay soil was packed to a hard smooth surface, and ordinarily it was circular with rocks placed around it. When I was in that land, I saw several places, especially in Samaria, where they had these threshing floors. The people were cutting the grain, not threshing it, when we were there in the spring; so we didn't see the threshing floor in operation. But there it was on top of a hill. They still do it the same way. After the grain was all cut, it was taken to the threshing floor. In the late afternoon a breeze would come up. It would blow until sundown and sometimes until midnight. Now as long as the breeze would blow they would thresh. Sheaves of grain were spread on the floor and trampled by oxen drawing a sled. Then the people took a flail and threw the grain up into the air so that the chaff would be blown away and the good grain would come down on the threshing floor. As long as the wind would blow, they would be there on the threshing floor. When the wind died down—whether it be at sundown, nine o'clock, midnight, or whatever time it was—they held a great religious feast. And at this season of the year all the families came up and camped around the threshing floor, which meant there were many people present. After the feast was over, the men would sleep around the grain. Since the threshing floor was circular, they would put their heads toward the grain and their feet would stick out like spokes. They slept that way to protect the grain from marauders or thieves who might break through and steal.

It was a time of feasting and thanking God for an abundant harvest. Several of the feast days of Israel—the feast of firstfruits and even Pentecost—were identified with that threshing floor. They would sing psalms praising God for a bountiful harvest. You can imagine them up there on that hill at night, looking out into the heavens and singing many of the psalms. When reading the psalms, note in particular how many of them deal with this particular religious feast.

With an understanding of the law of the kinsman-redeemer as it applied to the widow, and with the scene of the threshing floor in mind, let us move on.

Then Naomi her mother-in-law said unto her, My daughter, shall I not seek rest for thee, that it may be well with thee? [Ruth 3:1].

All during the harvest season Naomi had been watching out the window each afternoon and had seen Ruth and Boaz coming into Bethlehem. It had been about six weeks. Now the barley was gathered, and the wheat was gathered. Naomi notices that Ruth is very modest and is not making any claim upon this man at all. She also notices the obvious, that he is in love with her. And so Naomi asks Ruth if she should seek rest for her. And the rest, of course, is marriage. "Shall I seek a marriage for you?" You remember that at the very beginning she urged each of her daughters-in-law to stay in the land of Moab and find rest in her husband's house. So now she says she will seek rest for Ruth.

> **And now is not Boaz of our kindred, with whose maidens thou wast? Behold, he winnoweth barley tonight in the threshingfloor [Ruth 3:2].**

She says, "This man Boaz is your kinsman-redeemer. You have a right to claim him. In fact, Ruth, you must claim him as your kinsman-redeemer. I want you to go up to the threshing floor tonight and let him know."

> **Wash thyself therefore, and anoint thee, and put thy raiment upon thee, and get thee down to the floor: but make not thyself known unto the man, until he shall have done eating and drinking [Ruth 3:3].**

She tells Ruth to wait until the religious feast is over. Naomi says, "Now, Ruth, it's up to you to claim this man as your kinsman-redeemer." Ruth has been doing nothing in the way of claiming him, so Naomi is going to give her some very definite instructions. She tells her to do four things. I have felt that here is a picture of the sinner who comes to Jesus Christ. These are four steps that are essential for the sinner. The first one is this: Wash thyself. If you and I are going to come to Christ, we're told that it's "not by works of righteousness which we have done, but according to his mercy he saved us, by the washing of regeneration, and renewing of the Holy Ghost" (Titus 3:5). That's the reason our Lord said what He did to Nicodemus. "You may think you're a fine, religious man, and you are, but you need a bath—a spiritual bath. You need the washing of regeneration." And our Lord said to Nicodemus, ". . . Ye must be born again" (John 3:7). And, friend, if you are ever going to be fit for heaven, you must be born again. You must experience the new birth. Someone asked John Wesley why it was that he always preached on "ye must be born again" (for that was his favorite text). "Well," he said, "I'll tell you. The reason that I preach on 'ye must be born again' is because ye must be born again." You cannot get into heaven, friend, you cannot be saved until you have become a new creature in Christ Jesus. You and I are not fit for heaven until we have been born again, regenerated by the Holy Spirit. So Naomi tells Ruth, "You've been working hard out in the field. Wash thyself therefore." Now that's the first step that she is to take.

Now the second thing that Naomi tells Ruth to do is to anoint herself. After Ruth's first husband died, I suppose she put on widow's weeds and made no attempt to make herself attractive. But now Naomi realizes somebody is interested in Ruth, and so she tells her to get out that little bottle of perfume that she'd packed away and to use it generously. I can even suggest to you the name of the perfume that she used—"Midnight in Moab." And I want to tell you, that was an exotic perfume! And so Naomi says, "Anoint thee."

Now that corresponds also to our Christian experience. When you and I become children of God, we are babes, I grant that. But also we are brought to a full-grown status where we can understand divine truth. And there is something said to the believer about the anointing that he has. You and I have an anointing of the Holy Spirit. John tells us in 1 John 2:20, "But ye have an unction [anointing] from the Holy One, and ye know all things." That is, the Spirit of God is the One who can teach us all truth, and all of us need the teaching of the Spirit of God. That's the only way in the world we can ever understand the Word of

God, friend. The Spirit of God must teach us. And that's one of the neglected facts today. Right now in theological circles they are fighting like mad over the doctrine of inspiration. Now knowing that the Bible is inspired of God is very important. But you can believe in the plenary, verbal inspiration of the Scripture and still be ignorant of the Word of God. Why? You must recognize that you cannot bring to this Book human intellect alone and expect to understand it. You may understand facts; you may learn certain intellectual things; but only the Spirit of God can teach you spiritual things. Paul says in 1 Corinthians 2:9–10, "But as it is written, Eye hath not seen, nor ear heard, neither have entered into the heart of man, the things which God hath prepared for them that love him. But God hath revealed them unto us by his Spirit. . . ." The Spirit of God is able to teach us and is able to lead us and guide us into all truth. How important it is to have the Spirit of God as our teacher. "But God hath revealed them unto us by his Spirit: for the Spirit searcheth all things, yea, the deep things of God." We need to recognize that when we are born again we are given an anointing of the Spirit of God. It's mentioned again in 1 John 2:27. "But the anointing which ye have received of him abideth in you, and ye need not that any man teach you: but as the same anointing teacheth you of all things, and is truth, and is no lie, and even as it hath taught you, ye shall abide in him." This doesn't mean that you dispense with human learning or human teachers. You and I today are the beneficiaries of that which has been bequeathed to us by the godly men of the past whom the Spirit of God has taught. And God gives teachers to the church today. But not even the teachers nor all the wealth of material from the past can enlighten you unless the Spirit of God is your teacher. And so Ruth's second step was important. She was to wash herself and then to *anoint* herself.

Then the third thing: "Put thy raiment upon thee." And I think Naomi said to her, "Ruth, remember that little party dress that you used to wear when you and my son would go out together? You looked so pretty in it. And if Boaz fell in love with you when you were wearing those black, ugly widow's weeds, say, what'll he think when he sees you in this little party dress? So you put on that dress now that you put away and never intended to wear again."

This is the third step for the believer. When you and I come to Christ and accept Him as Savior, we are told that He becomes our righteousness. He not only subtracts our sin, He not only regenerates us and makes us a child of God, but He makes over to us His own righteousness. Actually, it's spoken of as a *robe* of righteousness. In Romans 3:22 it is described in a very wonderful way: "Even the righteousness of God which is by faith of Jesus Christ unto all and upon all them that believe: for there is no difference." Paul speaks of it as a garment that comes down over the sinner, covering him, so that God sees us in Christ, and His righteousness becomes our righteousness. We stand complete in Him—"accepted in the beloved" (Eph. 1:6). This is the robe of righteousness that we have today.

A book came out several years ago called *The Robe*. And there was an intelligent, dynamic young lady who was a member of my church. She came up to me one Sunday evening and said, "I've been reading a book, and it's a thriller." I asked her what it was. She said it was *The Robe*. I was a little discouraged when she said that. She asked if I'd read it, and I said, "Not exactly. I have the book, and I've looked through it, but I have not read it in any detail. In fact, I haven't cared to." And she looked at me in great amazement. She said, "Do you mean to tell me that you're not interested in what happened to that robe?" And I said, "Frankly, no. That seamless robe which Christ wore doesn't have a romantic history. The soldiers shot craps to see who would get it, and the fellow who won it must have been some big, burly Roman soldier. That's a semi-tropical country, and I happen to know it can get very hot there; he probably sweated out that robe in just a few weeks and then dropped it in some corner. Then a little servant maid came along, picked it up, held her nose, and dropped it in the trash can." This young lady was certainly shocked when I said that. She said, "That's terrible! According to the story, that robe had such a romantic history." I replied, "That robe had no romantic history at all. But there is one that does, and that's the robe of righteousness which Christ puts over the sinner who will trust Him."

And you and I cannot stand sufficient in ourselves; we stand complete in Him. Romans 4:25 tells us that it was Christ "who was delivered for our offences, and was raised again for our justification," in order that we might have a righteousness to stand before God. "For he hath made him to be sin for us . . . that we might be made the righteousness of God in him" (2 Cor. 5:21). And you and I stand clothed in that robe of righteousness, and that one really has a romantic history.

Now the fourth thing Naomi tells Ruth to do is to get down to the threshing floor and let Boaz know that she wants to claim him as her kinsman-redeemer.

> **And it shall be, when he lieth down, that thou shalt mark the place where he shall lie, and thou shalt go in, and uncover his feet, and lay thee down; and he will tell thee what thou shalt do [Ruth 3:4].**

And, friend, that's a very important step for you and me. That is a step that every sinner must take. Even in the church today are many folk who have joined the church, but they really never have received Jesus Christ. They never have gone down to the threshing floor and claimed Him as their Kinsman-Redeemer. And I'd like to ask: Have you really claimed Jesus Christ as your Savior? My friend, you do have to *claim* Him. The language of Scripture says to believe *upon* or believe *into* the Lord Jesus Christ. It must be an active faith, not a faith that stands on the sidelines and nods its head. It's an active faith that claims Him as Kinsman-Redeemer. He is our Savior. Oh, what a gift! ". . . The gift of God is eternal life through Jesus Christ our Lord" (Rom. 6:23).

Under the Mosaic Law, Ruth is not only entitled to and has a right to claim Boaz as her kinsman-redeemer, but she must claim him. And not only that, it's obvious that Boaz wants to be her kinsman-redeemer. The incident that is taking place makes possible the coming of Jesus Christ to this earth to be born in Bethlehem, for these events before us in the Book of Ruth are taking place in Bethlehem. This girl is going to obey her mother-in-law, and there's nothing wrong with what she is being instructed to do, as we shall see. She was asked to claim him; she had not claimed him.

Many people will tell you they believe in the facts concerning the coming of Christ into the world, but they've never yet accepted Christ.

Several years ago after speaking at a State Christian Endeavor convention in Fresno, California, as I walked across the auditorium with my coat slung over my shoulder, I saw a little delegation of college fellows approaching me. I recognized one of them as one of the officers of a Christian group at Fresno State College where I'd previously spoken. He said to me, "Dr. McGee, we have a young fellow here that we would like to have you talk to." And I said, "Well, fine. What about? What's the background?" And he said, "Well, this fellow agreed to come to the service tonight, and we'd hoped he would accept Christ, but he didn't, and so we just wish you'd talk with him." So I said to him, "Do you believe the Bible?" He said, "Yes." I was amazed. I had a notion he'd be the kind of college boy who'd want to argue about it. So I said, "Do you believe the story about the flood? That's sort of ridiculous about the flood, isn't it?" He said that it wasn't ridiculous to him. I said, "What about Jonah and the fish? Isn't that ridiculous?" He said, "No, not to me." And I said, "Well, do you believe it?" He said, "Yes." Well, I thought I'd have a boy who'd want to argue—they generally do—and I was prepared for it. Then I said to him, "Do you believe that Jesus Christ came into this world 1900 years ago as the Son of God and that He was virgin born?" He said, "Yes." "Do you believe He performed miracles?" He said, "Yes." "Do you believe He died on the cross for our sins?" And he said, "Yes." So I asked, "Do you believe He rose again bodily?" He said, "Yes." "Do you believe that He ascended into heaven?" He said, "Yes." Well, my gracious, the fellow believed everything that I asked him. And what do you do then? My course in personal evangelism never told me what to do next, so I just stood there, actually not knowing what step to take. Finally I just blurted out to him, "Young man, don't you want to take Christ as your Savior?" And he blurted right back and said, "Yes, I do." Well, the thing that had happened was that everybody, including myself, had wanted to argue with him about the Bible, but nobody ever stopped and said to him, "Get down to the threshing floor and accept Christ as your Savior." And this young man in a very wonderful way accepted Christ as his Savior. We got down on our knees in that great auditorium which was almost empty, and he accepted the Lord as his Savior. All he needed was just to get down to the threshing floor! And, frankly, I think there are a lot of folk like that today. Perhaps you are like that. You could be a church member, but really, have you ever gotten down to the threshing floor and personally, privately accepted Christ, claimed Him as your Savior from sin? When you trust Him, you will know what it is to pass from darkness to light.

Well, now, that's what Naomi tells Ruth to do.

And it shall be, when he lieth down, that thou shalt mark the place where he shall lie, and thou shalt go in, and uncover his feet, and lay thee down; and he will tell thee what thou shalt do.

And she said unto her, All that thou sayest unto me I will do.

And she went down unto the floor, and did according to all that her mother-in-law bade her [Ruth 3:4–6].

Now let me say that there is nothing questionable about the thing that
Naomi is asking her to do. To begin with, Naomi would never have
asked her to do it had it been improper. There have been those, however, who have criticized this, not understanding the threshing floor
or this peculiar law. You see, she must claim him as a kinsman-
redeemer. That's one thing. But this threshing floor was a public
place. The harvesters were there with their families. Naomi is saying
to Ruth, "Once they've finished the threshing for the evening and have
had their dinner, and a time for praise to God, a religious service, then
he will lie down. He'll put his head toward the grain and his feet out.
Now you go and put your feet toward his feet and pull his cloak up
over your feet, and then he'll let you know what to do." All of it would
be out in the public. The idea that something immoral is to take place
is due to our ignorance of the threshing floor during the harvest season.

> **And when Boaz had eaten and drunk, and his heart was
> merry, he went to lie down at the end of the heap of corn:
> and she came softly, and uncovered his feet, and laid her
> down.**

> **And it came to pass at midnight, that the man was
> afraid, and turned himself: and, behold, a woman lay at
> his feet [Ruth 3:7–8].**

You see, he got cold—the cloak had been pulled off him. He sat up,
reached down, and felt around down there, and lo, a woman was
there.

> **And he said, Who art thou? And she answered, I am
> Ruth thine handmaid: spread therefore thy skirt over
> thine handmaid; for thou art a near kinsman [Ruth
> 3:9].**

Personally, friend, I think this is one of the loveliest things that we have in the Word of God. Do you know what she is saying to him? She is saying, "I want you as my kinsman-redeemer, and I want to tell you so." That really changed the thinking of this man. I imagine he had been down in the dumps a little, but now he's a shouting Methodist. Listen.

And he said, Blessed be thou of the LORD, my daughter: for thou hast shewed more kindness in the latter end than at the beginning, inasmuch as thou followedst not young men, whether poor or rich [Ruth 3:10].

In other words, he said, "When you came here, it was obvious you were not husband-hunting." She had taken a very quiet, retired place. But now she is claiming Boaz as her kinsman-redeemer and, believe me, he is not reluctant to act in that capacity. And she's doing it in such a lovely fashion. She could have taken him into court. According to the Mosaic Law, you see, she could have called the elders of the city together and told Boaz outright, "I claim you as my kinsman-redeemer," and it would have been a legal matter. But Naomi suggested this way of doing it. She said, "There will be no question about the legality because this man obviously wants to be your kinsman-redeemer. All you have to do is to let him know that you're willing to claim him, that you want him as your kinsman-redeemer." And so she goes down to the threshing floor and in this very quiet, modest way lets him know she wants him as her kinsman-redeemer. Boaz immediately wants to claim her as his wife, because that's what he's been waiting to hear. This man really goes into action now because the way is clear and he is free to move; she has claimed him.

Thank God we have a Savior, and our relationship to Him is a love story. He loved us and He gave Himself for us in order that He might redeem us. What a wonderful, warm experience it is to know that we

have a Savior who died for us, who loves us, and lives for us today.
Now notice what Boaz says.

> **And now, my daughter, fear not; I will do to thee all that
> thou requirest: for all the city of my people doth know
> that thou art a virtuous woman [Ruth 3:11].**

And I'd have you note the reputation of this foreign girl who, under
ordinary circumstances, would have been an outcast in Bethlehem, an
outcast because the Mosaic Law shut out a Moabite. She'd been told
that a Moabite and an Ammonite could not enter into the congregation
of the Lord. She'd been coached by Naomi before they came to Bethlehem that there would be no possibility of her ever getting married, and
Ruth had accepted her status. I imagine that the town gossips had
looked her over very carefully at the beginning. I do not know what all
they had said, but I'm sure that among other things they'd said, "My,
this is certainly a pretty girl who has come back with Naomi. Certainly
she will be trying to get some of our young men." But she made no
attempt to do this. Instead she developed this wonderful reputation in
the town of Bethlehem.

Boaz continues.

> **And now it is true that I am thy near kinsman: howbeit
> there is a kinsman nearer than I [Ruth 3:12].**

How did he know about this? Well, he had already investigated. You
see, Boaz was ready to move the minute Ruth gave him the green light.
That was all he was waiting on. The fact that there was another kinsman nearer than he was had tied his hands.

Now this other kinsman could quite possibly be a richer man than
Boaz. Suppose Boaz had said to Ruth, back during the six weeks of
harvest, "Ruth, I want to be your kinsman-redeemer." And suppose
she had said, "Well, I thank you very much, but I don't want you. I am

claiming this other man when the time comes. He is a wealthier man, and I want to claim him as my kinsman-redeemer." Poor Boaz would have really been in a bad spot. He had to wait until she gave the indication that she wanted him. Now the minute she lets him know, he tells her, "The problem is there happens to be another kinsman closer than I am, and he has priority." In other words, he'll have to be dealt with first. And this other kinsman, I would assume, was a brother of Elimelech, an uncle of Ruth's first husband, whereas Boaz was probably a cousin of her first husband. And so he says, "I want to be your kinsman-redeemer, but first I'll have to see how this other man feels about you."

> Tarry this night, and it shall be in the morning, that if he will perform unto thee the part of a kinsman, well; let him do the kinsman's part: but if he will not do the part of a kinsman to thee, then will I do the part of a kinsman to thee, as the LORD liveth: lie down until the morning [Ruth 3:13].

In other words, Boaz is not sure what he will do if the other man wants to act as kinsman; but he has a plan that he's going to follow which he hopes will eliminate the other kinsman. And he emphasizes again and again this word *kinsman*. In the Hebrew it is *goel*, the kinsman-redeemer. He is the one to redeem Ruth's property, because she would inherit what her husband had; and he's the one to redeem her, you see. He has top priority. And Boaz tells Ruth to stay through the night. He did not want her to return to Bethlehem when it was dark —in that day the highways were no more safe than they are today. When we read about the period of the judges, we learn that people did not travel the main highways because they were not safe. Instead they'd take off across the fields. So what Boaz is doing is protecting this girl.

> **And she lay at his feet until the morning: and she rose up before one could know another. And he said, Let it not be known that a woman came into the floor [Ruth 3:14].**

Now the reason for that, again, is obvious. He did not want this other kinsman to know, because if he had any ideas about claiming Ruth as his wife, this would be something that would cause him to eliminate Boaz immediately. Boaz wants to handle this case himself, and he moves into the situation.

> **Also he said, Bring the veil that thou hast upon thee, and hold it. And when she held it, he measured six measures of barley, and laid it on her: and she went into the city [Ruth 3:15].**

In other words, he makes her a very generous gift.

> **And when she came to her mother-in-law, she said, Who art thou, my daughter? And she told her all that the man had done to her [Ruth 3:16].**

Other commentators, after whom I have read, seem to misinterpret her question. When Naomi asked, "Who art thou, my daughter?", they say since it was dark when she came up to the door Naomi wasn't sure who it was. Well, she at least knew that she was "my daughter." Of course she knew it was Ruth. We need to understand the context here. When Naomi sent her, I think Ruth was reluctant to go. I imagine she had said, "Oh, I don't want to claim him. You told me that if I came back here no one would be interested in me. I'm a Moabite, an outcast. I don't want to go down and claim Boaz." And Naomi said, "Look, I know he's interested in you, and I know he's in love with you, and I know he wants to marry you. Therefore, you do what I say." I think she almost had to push Ruth out of the house. So when Ruth returns the next morning, Naomi says, "Who art thou, my daughter?" Now let me put it in good ol' American: "Are you Mrs. Boaz or not?" In other words, "Was I right?" And, of course, she was right.

> **And she said, These six measures of barley gave he me; for he said to me, Go not empty unto thy mother-in-law.**
>
> **Then said she, Sit still, my daughter, until thou know how the matter will fall: for the man will not be in rest, until he have finished the thing this day [Ruth 3:17–18].**

Ruth, you can just sit down there in the rocking chair and wait. From here on Boaz will be the man of action. He will take care of this case. You can rest in him. The work of redemption is going to be his work.

Friend, it's wonderful to have a Savior in whom you can rest and know that He's your Redeemer. Oh, what a gift He is today! He has performed all the work of redemption. You and I are invited to enter into the rest of redemption because it is finished. You'll remember in His great high priestly prayer, He said to the Father, ". . . I have finished the work which thou gavest me to do" (John 17:4). Now that work was the work of redemption upon the cross. And when He was hanging there upon the cross, you will recall that He said, "It is finished" (John 19:30). And when He cried, "It is finished," then your redemption and my redemption was finished. He paid the penalty for your sin and my sin to such an extent that you cannot lift a little finger to add to your salvation. He has done it all.

> Jesus paid it all,
> All to Him I owe;
> Sin had left a crimson stain,
> He washed it white as snow.
> —E. M. Hall

The work of redemption is *His* work, and you and I are to enter into that perfect work of redemption which He accomplished for us. And there is a wonderful peace that will come to the heart that will trust Him, recognizing that He has completed it all. Frankly, God doesn't need your little effort and my little effort. God is not receiving anything from us toward our salvation. First of all, you and I haven't anything to offer. You and I are bankrupt. You and I have to come to Him to receive everything. I understand that that is the offense of the cross which Paul talks about in Galatians, because there are many people today who like to talk about their character, their family, or their church membership. They feel that church membership is synonymous with salvation, that if you're a member of a church in good and regular standing it means God has accepted you. There is nothing farther from the truth than that. God is not receiving your effort and my effort today. The work of redemption is His work in its entirety. He was lifted up upon the cross as the Son of Man. "And as Moses lifted up the serpent in the wilderness, even so must the Son of man be lifted up: That whosoever believeth in him should not perish, but have eternal life" (John 3:14–15). It is on the basis of His work upon the cross for you and me that God saves us. And that is the reason He came to this earth over 1900 years ago as a man. The writer to the Hebrews says, ". . . A body hast thou prepared me" (Heb. 10:5). Sacrifice and offering God did not want. All of the animal sacrifices in the Old Testament were merely pointing to the coming of Christ, given to prepare people for the coming of the Savior into the world. It's our acceptance and our reception of Him that saves us. He is the Savior. Actually even our faith doesn't save us. It is Christ who saves us. Spurgeon said, "It is not thy hold on Christ that saves thee; it is Christ. It is not thy joy in Christ that saves thee; it is Christ. It's not even thy faith in Christ, though that be the instrument; it is Christ's blood and merit." You see, faith merely enables us to lay hold of the salvation Christ has purchased for us. Now today you either trust Him or you don't trust Him.

There's no such thing as middle ground today. You're either resting in Him or you are trying to earn your own salvation.

And so Ruth 3 concludes with Naomi saying to Ruth, "The man will not be in rest, until he have finished the thing this day." And she said to Ruth, "Sit still, my daughter. There's nothing more for you to do. When you claimed him as your redeemer, that's all he asked you to do. The work of redemption is his work."

CHAPTER 4

THEME: In the heart and home of Boaz

R uth has come all the way from the land of Moab into the heart and home of Boaz. And we who were at one time strangers, far from God, without hope in the world, now have been made nigh by the blood of Christ. We today are in the family of God; we are in His heart. And one of these days we are going to be in His home. What a glorious, wonderful prospect we have of someday being with Him!

In this chapter we will see the work of Boaz. He has had to stand aside with his arms folded, but now he is free to move because Ruth has claimed him as her kinsman-redeemer. And I say this reverently to you, my friend: Christ, like Boaz, is not free to move in your behalf until you claim Him as your Kinsman-Redeemer. Christ died on the cross for you; He went through hell for you; and He even today stands at the door of your heart and knocks, saying, "Behold, I stand at the door, and knock: if any man hear my voice, and open the door, I will come in to him, and will sup with him, and he with me" (Rev. 3:20). But He won't crash the door. You will have to invite Him in. God offers the gift of eternal life in Christ Jesus, but you have to reach out your hand and take it by faith. By faith you receive Christ.

Boaz is ready to act in the capacity of kinsman-redeemer. Ruth is to wait and let him be the one to make all the arrangements. He is the one now who will step out into the open and claim her, actually jeopardizing everything that he has and everything that he is. But he wants her;

he loves her. This is the great message of this book: redemption is a
romance; because God loves us He redeemed us.

> **Then went Boaz up to the gate, and sat him down there:**
> **and, behold, the kinsman of whom Boaz spake came by;**
> **unto whom he said, Ho, such a one! turn aside, sit down**
> **here. And he turned aside, and sat down [Ruth 4:1].**

"Boaz went up to the gate." Why did he go there? Well, simply because
the gate served as the courthouse. That's where court convened. In our
American way of life, in the past at least, the custom was to build the
courthouse in the center of town, put a square around it, and actually
build the town around it. In the state of Texas where I was born that
was done in nearly all of the county seats.

In the days of Boaz it was different. You see, many of the towns
were walled in order to protect the citizens from any marauder or enemy that would attack from the outside. The cities were very
compact—streets were narrow, and houses were crowded close together. You can see that today in Bethlehem and in Jerusalem. Most of
the old cities over there reveal this. Bethlehem in Ruth's day was that
kind of place, so that the gate was the place where everybody came in
or went out. Like the courthouse in the old days, especially on a Satur-
day, if you wanted to see anybody in the county, you'd just go to the
courthouse square, and the chances were you would see him. Well,
here in the Old Testament times they went to the gate. Now Boaz went
to the gate for two reasons. It was where court convened, and he was
going to take this other kinsman to court. The second reason is that he
knows the other man will come in or out of that gate sooner or later that
day. So he went to the gate, sat down, and waited there for him. Now I
do not know how long he waited—it probably seemed a long time to
Boaz—but finally the man he wanted to see came by. Now this man
was a kinsman to Ruth and was nearer than Boaz. I do not know the
relationship. In these early days they did not express relationships

specifically. You just couldn't narrow it down to a second cousin or a kissing cousin. A man was either kin to you or he wasn't kin to you. And the same word would be used for a brother or an uncle or some other relationship. I assume that this other man was a brother of Elimelech, Naomi's husband, which made him an uncle of Ruth's first husband. So when Boaz sees him, he says, "Ho, such a one!" Now the question arises, didn't he know him by name? And I think the answer is yes, he knew him by name. We've all done something similar, I'm sure. Even though we know the person's name, just on the spur of the moment, we may address him without using his name. And Boaz, in the excitement of the situation, fails to call him by name. I'm confident Boaz knew him. They both lived there in Bethlehem, and they were related apparently by blood. So this other kinsman came and sat down. He responded to what was almost a command from Boaz. And I think that his reaction would have been simply this: "What in the world has happened to Boaz? Here it is the harvesting season and we're all busy in the fields, and he is detaining me. He must have something very important to discuss. This is really unusual." So the kinsman, if for no other reason than that of curiosity, wants to know what it is that's on the mind of Boaz.

And he took ten men of the elders of the city, and said, Sit ye down here. And they sat down [Ruth 4:2].

These ten men were elders, we're told, and they were the ones who constituted the judges. This is the courthouse, and court's in session. You will find way back in the Book of Genesis, that the men who came to the city of Sodom found Lot was sitting at the gate. Lot had become a petty judge there in the city of Sodom. Even that far back the city gate served as the courthouse, and the men who sat in the gate were the judges. Now Boaz has called the court into session, and they're ready to hear the case. And Boaz is ready to state it, by the way. Notice the strategy of this man. It's quite remarkable.

And he said unto the kinsman, Naomi, that is come again out of the country of Moab, selleth a parcel of land, which was our brother Elimelech's [Ruth 4:3].

Now notice the approach Boaz makes. Although he is primarily interested in Ruth, he doesn't even mention her at first. And does this verse mean that Boaz was Elimelech's brother also? Not in the Hebrew. "Our brother Elimelech" would mean "our near relative." Apparently there was a difference between these two men's relationships to Elimelech, or one kinsman wouldn't have been nearer than the other. He had to be nearer than Boaz was. In his approach, Boaz says that there's a piece of property involved. We have already seen that there was a law pertaining to property which involved the kinsman-redeemer. This law could be put into effect when a person's property fell into the hands of others through varied circumstances. In the case of Naomi, she and her family had left during a famine. When she came back, she had nothing. She could not retrieve her property. She would have to wait until the Year of Jubilee, and I assume that was a long way off. But now what is going to happen? Will a kinsman-redeemer come forward? Boaz is calling this other kinsman's attention, not to the person of Ruth, but to the property that belonged to Elimelech. He wants to know whether this other kinsman will redeem that property. I think that it's a logical step. Property had to be redeemed before a person could be redeemed.

Now Boaz says,

And I thought to advertise thee, saying, Buy it before the inhabitants, and before the elders of my people. If thou wilt redeem it, redeem it: but if thou wilt not redeem it, then tell me, that I may know: for there is none to redeem it beside thee; and I am after thee. And he said, I will redeem it [Ruth 4:4].

In other words, Boaz gives this man the priority that belongs to him. And the question is: Does this man want to be the redeemer? Will he redeem this property in order that it might be given to Naomi before the Year of Jubilee? Now the very interesting thing is that this other kinsman responds in the affirmative. He says, "I will redeem it." Apparently he was a generous man, and he was willing to perform the part of a kinsman in this connection. And I take it that if a man refused to be a kinsman, it brought upon him a certain amount of criticism, in fact, it brought a degree of disgrace. And I think that when this man agreed to redeem the property, Boaz's heart must have gone way down into his sock. But he would not give up. He had prepared for this eventuality, and he was ready now to reveal his hand, and to show that there was more to this case than just a piece of property.

> **Then said Boaz, What day thou buyest the field of the hand of Naomi, thou must buy it also of Ruth the Moabitess, the wife of the dead, to raise up the name of the dead upon his inheritance [Ruth 4:5].**

It's as if Boaz said, "Well, I forgot to tell you that there is in connection with this property a little hurdle that you'll have to get over. You see, there is now a woman by the name of Ruth. She's a Moabitess, and she's connected with the property because she happened to marry a son of Elimelech. And now that both he and Elimelech are dead, she'll be the one to inherit this land. So the day that you redeem this property, you've also got to redeem this woman; that is, you'll have to step in and marry Ruth, because she's tied to this property." And I think Boaz made the problem very clear. And you'll notice he let the man know the nationality of the woman involved. "She is a *Moabitess*." Now the Mosaic Law says very specifically in Deuteronomy 23:3, "An Ammonite or Moabite shall not enter into the congregation of the LORD." It would mean that if this man brought Ruth into the congregation of the Lord, it would jeopardize his own property. Now Boaz will not mind doing that. To tell the truth, Boaz will be delighted to do that. He loves her and he is willing to make whatever sacrifice is involved. But this other man doesn't even know her. All he knows is that she is a woman of Moab. Regardless of what he may have heard, he certainly is not interested in marrying her, and he makes that very clear.

> **And the kinsman said, I cannot redeem it for myself, lest I mar mine own inheritance: redeem thou my right to thyself; for I cannot redeem it [Ruth 4:6].**

Now I assume that this other kinsman was already married. It's quite possible that he had grown children the age of Boaz, and that his children were married. His property already would be allotted to his children. To marry this woman of Moab would jeopardize everything that he owned. He would be risking everything by marrying Ruth and bringing her into the congregation of the Lord. Very candidly, this other kinsman probably was right in what he said, that he could not redeem the property and Ruth because his own inheritance would be marred. Then he tells Boaz, "You go ahead and take my right of redemption to yourself if this is what you want to do."

Now I have attempted to lift out of this little book some of the great spiritual lessons that are here—and there are many. The kinsman-redeemer is one of the most marvelous pictures that we have of our Lord Jesus Christ who redeemed us. In other words, as we said at the very beginning, this story is a picture of our redemption. This is the way our Kinsman-Redeemer has acted in our behalf.

Also we have a marvelous picture in this other kinsman. What does he represent? I personally think that he represents the Mosaic Law. To begin with, he's nameless. The Law could not redeem us. It was impossible for the Law to redeem us. That's made very clear in the New Testament. "Therefore by the deeds of the law there shall no flesh be justified in his sight: for by the law is the knowledge of sin" (Rom. 3:20). The Law was never given to be a redeemer. The Law was given to reveal man's true condition. Paul calls it a ministration of condemnation (2 Cor. 3:9) and a ministration of death (2 Cor. 3:7). The Law was never a savior. The Law actually condemned us rather than saved us. It was given as an attempt to control the old nature. There was really never anyone who got saved by keeping the precepts of the Law. It was only as they brought the sacrifice that pointed to Christ that they were ever made acceptable to God. And that's the reason the great Day of Atonement was so important. It covered the sins of ignorance for everyone in Israel. On that day their attention was called to the fact that they needed a Savior even to deliver them from the Law. Like the other kinsman, the Law was unable to save. The other kinsman said it would mar his own inheritance. And the law would have to lower its standards if it saved you or me, friend. I hear a great many people who talk rather foolishly about keeping the Law. They say, "I live by the Ten Commandments," or "I live by the Sermon on the Mount." Well, do you? There are those that say, "That's my religion." If that is your religion, I have a question for you: How are you getting along? Are you keeping it? "Oh," somebody says, "I'm trying mighty hard." A very prominent businessman told me that years ago in Nashville, Tennessee. Well, you can't find anywhere in the Sermon on the Mount or in the Ten Commandments or in the Mosaic system where it says you are to try. God says, "Do these things." He didn't say anything in the world about trying. You can't come halfway. This other kinsman, who symbolizes the Law, said, "I cannot redeem." The Law cannot redeem you. You have to have somebody who will love you, friend, and somebody to pay the penalty of your sins. That's the only way you'll ever get saved. You cannot measure up to God's standard. You and I are way short of God's standard. We need today a Kinsman-Redeemer who loves us and who was not only willing to risk everything, but who actually gave His life. When He took our place, He paid an awful penalty. He died upon the cross for our sins.

In order to make a contract or agreement binding, it was necessary to follow an unusual procedure.

> **Now this was the manner in former time in Israel concerning redeeming and concerning changing, for to confirm all things; a man plucked off his shoe, and gave it to his neighbour: and this was a testimony in Israel [Ruth 4:7].**

You'll recall that when we looked at this law back in Deuteronomy 25, it said that the woman was to take off his shoe and spit in his face. Well, I'm glad Boaz didn't spit in his face here, but he did take off the shoe. And we see that Boaz has taken the place of Ruth in this entire transaction; he is acting for her. On her behalf he takes off the shoe of the other man, and this girl is now to become his wife. Now I have given names to nearly everyone in this little Book of Ruth, and I have a name for this other kinsman. He's Old Barefoot. He lost his shoe. You know, only the Gospel has ever put shoes on our feet. "And your feet shod with the preparation of the gospel of peace" (Eph. 6:15). The old Law, my friend, is barefoot. It cannot save you at all.

> **Therefore the kinsman said unto Boaz, Buy it for thee. So he drew off his shoe.**
>
> **And Boaz said unto the elders, and unto all the people, Ye are witnesses this day, that I have bought all that was Elimelech's, and all that was Chilion's and Mahlon's, of the hand of Naomi.**
>
> **Moreover Ruth the Moabitess, the wife of Mahlon, have I purchased to be my wife, to raise up the name of the dead upon his inheritance, that the name of the dead be not cut off from among his brethren, and from the gate of his place: ye are witnesses this day [Ruth 4:8–10].**

First he redeems the property, you see. Then he is also the redeemer for Ruth. He acts the part of a kinsman and makes her his wife. He does it because he's in love with her. Since Boaz depicts the Lord Jesus Christ, our Kinsman-Redeemer, it is very important to see that He has acted in our behalf. Now Boaz calls the people to witness the fact that he not only has redeemed the property, but he has also redeemed Ruth, the widow of Mahlon.

> **And all the people that were in the gate, and the elders, said, We are witnesses. The LORD make the woman that is come into thine house like Rachel and like Leah, which two did build the house of Israel: and do thou worthily in Ephratah, and be famous in Beth-lehem [Ruth 4:11].**

These people of Bethlehem are rejoicing in this because—as we've been told twice—this girl, though a foreigner, an outsider, has made a wonderful name for herself in Bethlehem. It was obvious that she, as a Moabite, had made a tremendous sacrifice to trust God as her Savior. And she didn't spend her time running around chasing every man in the community, and Boaz had noted that, you remember.

The impression you get from some girls today is that they start out as soon as they are able, and they chase the boys until finally they run one down and marry him. And then we wonder why those marriages don't work out. I risk being thought archaic for saying this, but I believe it is still the prerogative of the man to do the chasing. The man is always the deliverer, and the woman is the receiver. God made them that way. And that's why He says to the man, "Husbands, love your wives" (Eph. 5:25). He didn't turn that around and instruct the wife to love the husband. Somebody asks, "Well, isn't she supposed to?" Of course she is, but she's a responder. She is to *respond* to him. If he loves her, then she will love him. If he treats her harshly and cruelly, she will become cold and indifferent, and love will die. In the majority of cases—and over the years I have counselled literally hundreds of cases that have to do with marriage problems—the man is to blame. You see, he is the one who is responsible because he is to be the leader.

As a man chooses a woman for his bride, and as Boaz claimed Ruth, so Christ came to this earth for His bride. He is the One who demonstrated His love by dying for us. And we are the responder—we are to respond to His love. We are to receive Him as Savior, then come to know Him. Oh, friend, that should be the ambition of every Christian—to *know* Him! It is sad that a great many people make a trip to Bethlehem once a year and look in a manger. He's not there, friend. Although He did come as a baby, He hasn't been a baby for a long time. Then at Easter they go look in an empty tomb, and He's not there either. He's the Man in the glory today. And Paul could write that his ambition was, "That I may know him, and the power of his resurrection, and the fellowship of his sufferings" (Phil. 3:10). That was the goal of this man. Oh, that we might know Him, our Kinsman-Redeemer, and love Him because He first loved us.

And now all the people of Bethlehem are joyful over the events that are taking place in the life of Boaz. And they continue to express this.

> **And let thy house be like the house of Pharez, whom Tamar bare unto Judah, of the seed which the LORD shall give thee of this young woman.**
>
> **So Boaz took Ruth, and she was his wife: and when he went in unto her, the LORD gave her conception, and she bare a son.**
>
> **And the women said unto Naomi, Blessed be the LORD, which hath not left thee this day without a kinsman, that his name may be famous in Israel [Ruth 4:12–14].**

The women said this to Naomi because, you see, Naomi needed a kinsman to carry on the line of Elimelech. Now it will be carried on through Boaz.

We have a Kinsman today, and that's the most wonderful news we can have, friend. Look today at this poor, sin-stained world. It is puzzled, not knowing where to turn. And look at the faces. I've looked into the faces of literally thousands of people in downtown Los Angeles and elsewhere. If they are happy, their faces don't reveal it. The children appear happy but not the older folk. Their lives seem almost aimless, without hope, without God in the world. They need a Kinsman. It's tragic to see people celebrate Christmas or Easter or anything that relates to Christ without knowing He is their Kinsman and without having received Him as their Kinsman-Redeemer.

And he shall be unto thee a restorer of thy life, and a nourisher of thine old age: for thy daughter-in-law, which loveth thee, which is better to thee than seven sons, hath born him.

And Naomi took the child, and laid it in her bosom, and became nurse unto it [Ruth 4:15–16].

This child, you see, is Naomi's grandson. And how precious he is to her.

And the women her neighbours gave it a name, saying, There is a son born to Naomi; and they called his name Obed: he is the father of Jesse, the father of David [Ruth 4:17].

Naomi's neighbors, seeing her great love for the child, named him Obed, meaning "servant" or "worshiper." Although he was of no blood kin to Naomi, he was legally her grandson. Undoubtedly, he became a little servant to Naomi in her old age and took the place left vacant by the death of her husband and two sons. Her estate, of course, would go to this son of Boaz and Ruth.

He is a worshiper of the living and the true God.

Now we're given Obed's genealogy. Obed is the father of Jesse. And who is Jesse? He is the father of David.

> **Now these are the generations of Pharez: Pharez begat Hezron,**
>
> **And Hezron begat Ram, and Ram begat Amminadab,**
>
> **And Amminadab begat Nahshon, and Nahshon began Salmon,**
>
> **And Salmon begat Boaz, and Boaz begat Obed,**
>
> **And Obed begat Jesse, and Jesse begat David [Ruth 4:18–22].**

In one sense this genealogy that concludes the Book of Ruth is just about as important as any portion of the Old Testament. Do you know why? Because this little book and this genealogy are what connect the family of David with the tribe of Judah. Without it we would have no written record of the connection. This makes the little Book of Ruth very important, as you can see, because it fits into God's plan and into God's scheme.

As a fitting climax for the little Book of Ruth, let us look further at the kinsman-redeemer as he pictures the Lord Jesus Christ. In what sense did our Lord fulfill that which the kinsman-redeemer represents? There were several requirements a man had to meet in order to qualify as a kinsman-redeemer. We shall look at several of them.

First of all, he must be a *near kinsman*. Second, he must be *willing* to redeem. The third requirement is that the kinsman-redeemer must be *able* to redeem. And the fourth, the kinsman-redeemer must be *free* himself. And finally, the redeemer must have the *price* of redemption. He must be able to pay in legal tender that which is acceptable.

Now Boaz was able to meet all of these conditions as the kinsman-redeemer of Ruth. And the Lord Jesus Christ as our Kinsman-Redeemer, and the Kinsman-Redeemer of the world, meets all these requirements also.

First of all, let's consider that the kinsman-redeemer must be a *near* kinsman. That seems to be obvious and needs no proof. In fact, that is the reason Boaz could act. He said, "I am your near kinsman." Presented to us from beginning to end is the fact that Boaz was related to the family of Elimelech. And the Lord Jesus Christ is our Kinsman-Redeemer. He is a near kinsman. He is the One who took upon Himself our humanity. "Forasmuch then as the children are partakers of flesh and blood, he also himself likewise took part of the same; that through death he might destroy him that had the power of death, that is, the devil; And deliver them who through fear of death were all their lifetime subject to bondage. For verily he took not on him the nature of angels; but he took on him the seed of Abraham" (Heb. 2:14–16). The Lord Jesus Christ came into our human family, "he took on him the seed of Abraham," we're told here. We are also told that He ". . . can have compassion on the ignorant, and on them that are out of the way; for that he himself also is compassed with infirmity" (Heb. 5:2). He knew what it was to be a man. "But when the fulness of the time was come, God sent forth his Son, made of a woman, made under the law, To redeem them that were under the law, that we might receive the adoption of sons" (Gal. 4:4–5). He was born of a woman, born under the Law. You see, He came down and took upon Himself our humanity, and He became a man. And it was for the joy that was set before Him that He came down to this earth and entered into the human family. That, my friend, is one of the greatest encouragements that I could have today. If you could persuade me that God had not become man (you cannot persude me of that, by the way, but if you could), then, I say it reverently and with some thought, I'd turn my back on God. However, you cannot persuade me of this, and I'll not turn my back on Him, because over 1900 years ago He came down and took upon Himself my humanity. And He suffered down here; He bled and died. He is able to help me today because He knows me and He knows you. He knows you better than your friends know you, than your relatives know you, than your wife or husband knows you. He knows you better than you know yourself. He knows you today, and He can help you today because of that. Because God became man and took my humanity upon Himself, then, although there are many experiences in this life I cannot explain, and do not know why certain things happen today, I accept them. Since He became a man, and since He found it necessary to come down to this earth to suffer and to bleed and to die for the sins of the world—which is in the plan and program of God—I know that life has some high and holy purpose. I'm going to get up and brush myself off when I fall again, and I'm going to continue right on through life because I know that we're pressing ". . . toward the mark for the prize of the high calling of God in Christ Jesus" (Phil. 3:14).

Christ's humanity has been expressed in a lovely little poem by Jean Ingelow:

> O, God, O Kinsman loved, but not enough!
>   O Man, with eyes majestic after death,
> Whose feet have toiled along our pathways rough,
>   Whose lips drawn human breath!
>
> By that one likeness which is ours and Thine,
>   By that one nature which doth hold us kin;
> By that high heaven where sinless Thou dost shine,
>   To draw us sinners in.

Anselm, one of the great saints of the period before the Middle Ages, in his book, *Cur Deus Homo*, that is, *Why God Became Man*, reduces to one well-defined point the problem of why God became a man. That point is defined by one word: *redemption*. The Lord Jesus Christ took upon Himself our humanity and our flesh that He might be our Kinsman-Redeemer on this first point: He is our near Kinsman!

Not only must a kinsman-redeemer be a near kinsman, but he must also be *willing* to redeem. You will recall that Naomi's other kinsman was not willing to redeem. He very frankly told Boaz, "I'll mar my own inheritance. I cannot redeem it. You redeem my right for yourself." And Boaz was willing—not only willing—he *wanted* to redeem it, because he loved Ruth. And you and I today have a Kinsman who loves us. Why? There's no explanation in us. Paul said in Romans 3:24: "Being justified freely by his grace through the redemption that is in Christ Jesus." "Freely" means without a cause. He didn't find any cause in us at all. But He loves us, and He's a willing Redeemer. The writer to the Hebrews says, "Looking unto Jesus the author and finisher of our faith; who for the joy that was set before him endured the cross, despising the shame, and is set down at the right hand of the throne of God" (Heb. 12:2). And so we find that the Lord Jesus, as our Kinsman-Redeemer, was willing to redeem us. He wanted to redeem us and He loves us today. He was a willing sacrifice. It has been suggested by some, and wrongly so, that because Jesus was a willing sacrifice, He was a suicide like Socrates. That's a blasphemous statement, but some of the liberals have made it, as they have made other blasphemous statements. Although His death was not a suicide, He certainly was willing to die—you see, He loved us! Many years ago down in Houston, Texas, when a boarding house caught on fire, a woman broke through the lines and went into that house. It collapsed, and she was burned to death. The headlines read: "Poor Wretch Dies: Suicide." Later the newspaper corrected it, and printed an apology. Do you know why? It was because when workmen were digging around in the rubble, they found in a back room, a little iron bed, and in that little iron bed was a baby, *her* baby. She entered that burning building to save her baby. She wasn't a suicide. She loved that baby and wanted to save her child. The Lord Jesus was a willing Redeemer, friend, very willing, and it was because He loved us.

Third, a kinsman-redeemer must be *able* to redeem. I am sure that Naomi had some poor kinfolk there in Bethlehem—we all have poor kinfolk, haven't we? It might have been that one night after Naomi had come back from Moab that these poor kinfolk came over, they all got out their handkerchiefs and they wept. They said, "Naomi, we feel sorry for you, but we can't help you. In fact, we're in pretty bad shape ourselves. We can't even help ourselves." It's *nice* to have folk sympathize with you, but it's *wonderful* to have a kinsman who is able to write a check that doesn't bounce, and to have that kinsman come along and say, "I'll redeem you." Well, you and I have a Kinsman-Redeemer. One of the things that is said about Him is that He is able to redeem. Have you ever noticed the many times in the New Testament that it says the Lord Jesus is able? He is able. "Wherefore he is able also to save them to the uttermost that come unto God by him, seeing he ever liveth to make intercession for them" (Heb. 7:25). He is our great Kinsman-Redeemer with the ability to save. That, of course, was true of Boaz. He was called a mighty man of wealth. There was never any question about his ability. And, friend, there's never a question about whether the Lord Jesus can redeem. Job could say, "For I know that my redeemer liveth, and that he shall stand at the latter day upon the earth" (Job 19:25). I can say today that I know that my Redeemer liveth, because He is right now at God's right hand, and He stood one day upon this earth. In fact, He hung one day upon a cross that He might redeem us from sin. He is able to save. And we're told today that God has highly exalted Him and given Him a name above every name, and that some day every tongue must confess and every knee must bow to Him (Phil. 2:9–11). He is able to save. And may I say, He is able to save *you*. The question is: Has He saved you? He wants to, and He will if you'll come to Him.

BIBLIOGRAPHY

(Recommended for Further Study)

Barber, Cyril J. *Ruth*. Chicago, Illinois: Moody Press, 1983.

Davis, John J. *Conquest and Crisis—Studies in Joshua, Judges, and Ruth*. Grand Rapids, Michigan: Baker Book House, 1969.

Enns, Paul P. *Ruth*. Grand Rapids, Michigan: Zondervan Publishing House, 1981.

Gaebelein, Arno C. *The Annotated Bible*. Vol. 2. Neptune, New Jersey: Loizeaux Brothers, 1917.

Grant, F.W. *Numerical Bible*. Vol. 2. Neptune, New Jersey: Loizeaux Brothers, 1891.

Gray, James M. *Synthetic Bible Studies*. Westwood, New Jersey: Fleming H. Revell Co., 1906.

Jensen, Irving L. *Judges & Ruth, A Self-Study Guide*. Chicago, Illinois: Moody Press, 1968.

McGee, J. Vernon. *Ruth, The Romance of Redemption*. Pasadena, California: Thru the Bible Books, 1943.

Mackintosh, C.H. *The Mackintosh Treasury: Miscellaneous Writings*. Neptune, New Jersey: Loizeaux, n.d.

Ridout, Samuel. *Lectures on the Books of Judges and Ruth*. Neptune, New Jersey: Loizeaux Brothers, n.d.